DIGITAL SAT®

ULTIMATE EXAM PREP

2025

A Concise Yet Comprehensive Guide
to Maximize Your Studying and
Ace the Digital SAT® on Your First Try

JUPITER DIGITAL EXAM PREP

TABLE OF CONTENTS

INTRODUCTION

INTRODUCTION TO THE DIGITAL SAT®

Welcome to your personal guide for the Digital SAT®! As you begin your journey towards college admissions, grasping the significance and format of the Digital SAT® is essential. This guide aims to offer you the information and effective strategies to help you succeed in this important milestone of your academic journey.

The SAT® originally named the Scholastic Aptitude Test has always played a role in the U.S. College admissions process. Managed by the College Board, this standardized test evaluates students' preparedness for education by assessing their abilities in reading, writing and math. In times there has been a shift in the SAT® from its traditional paper-based version to a digital platform. This change mirrors the changing landscape of education and technology ensuring that the SAT® remains relevant and accessible to students in today's era.

The Digital SAT® presents benefits compared to its paper-based predecessor. Through its format students can enjoy a user-friendly testing interface with convenient features like a timer, calculator, and reference materials at their disposal. Additionally, the digital platform enables score processing delivering results to students within days, then weeks.

Also, the College Board has put in place improved security measures to uphold the exams' integrity and deter cheating.

As you get ready, for the Digital SAT® it's important to understand the exams format and content. The Digital SAT® is split into two parts; Evidence Based Reading and Writing (EBRW) and Math. The EBRW section includes a Reading Test and a Writing and Language Test, which evaluate your comprehension, analysis and editing skills. The Math section, where you can use a calculator, tests your problem-solving abilities and grasp of concepts.

To achieve your score on the Digital SAT® it's crucial to approach your preparation. This guide serves as your all tool providing coverage of each exam section along with effective strategies, advice, and practice materials. By committing to a organized study plan and utilizing the information in this guide you can develop the confidence and skills needed to excel on test day.

One of the advantages of this guide is its focus on practicality. Preparing for the Digital SAT® can feel overwhelming. We aim to offer advice and effective strategies to support your study efforts. In this guide you'll discover explanations of concepts step, by step methods for approaching various question types and insights into the exams structure and scoring.

To get the most out of this resource we suggest taking an approach to studying. Start by understanding the guides layout and chapter topics. Set study goals. Create a schedule that allows ample time for each exam section. As you progress through the chapters practice with the questions provided and use the answer explanations to strengthen your grasp of the material.

Beyond content review this guide also presents test taking tips and stress management strategies to enhance your performance, on test day. Whether it's navigating the interface or managing time effectively during the exam these techniques will boost your confidence. Help you tackle the Digital SAT® with ease.

As you start on this journey keep in mind that preparing for the Digital SAT® goes beyond memorizing facts and formulas. It's about honing your thinking skills, problem solving abilities and the resilience to face challenges directly. By embracing the learning process and dedicating yourself to practice and self-assessment you will not enhance your chances of success on the Digital SAT® but also develop important skills that will benefit you in your academic and professional endeavors. So let's delve into the world of the Digital SAT® together! With dedication, persistence, and effective strategies you can unleash your potential. Attain the scores necessary to pursue your college aspirations. Remember, triumph on the Digital SAT® is within your grasp and this guide is here to assist you every step of the way.

HOW TO USE THIS GUIDE

Welcome to your journey towards mastering the Digital SAT®! This study guide is designed to be your comprehensive companion, providing you with the knowledge, strategies, and practice you need to excel on the exam. Whether you're a first-time test-taker or looking to improve your previous scores, this guide will help you navigate the digital format and build the skills necessary for success.

Understanding the Guide's Structure

To get the most out of this study guide, it's essential to understand its structure and how to use it effectively. The guide is divided into five main parts, each focusing on a different aspect of the Digital SAT®:

1. Understanding the Digital SAT®
2. Evidence-Based Reading and Writing
3. Math
4. Test-Taking Strategies and Tips
5. Practice Tests and Solutions

Each part contains several chapters that delve into specific topics, providing in-depth explanations, examples, and practice exercises. This structure allows you to focus on the areas where you need the most improvement and to progress at your own pace.

Creating a Personalized Study Plan

One of the most critical aspects of preparing for the Digital SAT® is developing a study plan that caters to your unique needs and goals. The first step in creating your personalized study plan is to thoroughly review the guide's table of contents. Take note of the sections that cover topics you find particularly challenging or areas where you know you need to improve. For example, if you've struggled with Math in the past, you may want to prioritize the chapters that focus on algebraic concepts, problem-solving strategies, and data analysis.

Once you've identified the sections that are most relevant to your needs, consider your current skill level and the amount of time you have before the exam. Be honest with yourself about your strengths and weaknesses, and set realistic goals based on your starting point. If you're a few months away from the test date, you may have more flexibility to dedicate time to each section. However, if you're on a tighter timeline, you'll need to be more strategic about how you allocate your study hours.

To make your study plan manageable and less overwhelming, break it down into smaller, focused chunks. For instance, you might dedicate one week to mastering linear equations and systems, followed by a week of practice exercises related to that topic. As you plan out your study schedule, be sure to allow for regular review sessions to reinforce what you've learned and identify any areas that need further attention.

It's also important to build flexibility into your study plan. Life can be unpredictable, and there may be times when you need to adjust your schedule. Don't be too hard on yourself if you miss a day or two of studying; just make sure to get back on track as soon as possible. Remember, consistency is key, and even short study sessions can make a big difference over time.

As you progress through your study plan, take time to celebrate your achievements and milestones along the way. Recognizing your hard work and progress can help keep you motivated and focused on your ultimate goal of succeeding on the Digital SAT®.

Engaging with the Material

Actively engaging with the study material is essential to making the most of your Digital SAT® preparation. Simply reading through the chapters and examples without truly processing the information will likely not lead to the results you're seeking. Instead, approach each study session with the intention of fully immersing yourself in the content.

One effective way to engage with the material is to take notes as you read. Jot down key concepts, formulas, and strategies in your own words. This process of summarizing and rephrasing the information can help you internalize it more effectively. Additionally, highlighting or underlining important passages can make it easier to locate key ideas when you're reviewing later.

As you encounter examples throughout the guide, resist the temptation to immediately look at the provided explanations. Instead, challenge yourself to solve each example problem on your own first. This hands-on practice will help you develop your problem-solving skills and give you a more accurate sense of your current understanding. Once you've given the example your best effort, carefully review the explanations to see how your approach compares to the recommended solution.

Another way to actively engage with the material is to create your own questions or problems based on the concepts you're learning. This can help you think more deeply about the topics and explore different ways of applying your knowledge. You can also seek out additional resources, such as online videos or supplementary practice problems, to reinforce your understanding and expose yourself to a variety of question styles.

Don't be afraid to spend extra time on concepts that are particularly challenging for you. The effort you put in now will pay off when you're facing similar questions on the actual Digital SAT®.

Utilizing Practice Exercises

The practice exercises at the end of each chapter are a crucial component of your Digital SAT® study plan. These exercises give you the opportunity to apply the concepts, strategies, and techniques you've learned in a format that closely resembles the actual exam. By working through these practice questions regularly, you'll be able to reinforce your understanding, identify areas where you need additional support, and build your confidence for test day.

To get the most out of the practice exercises, it's important to create an environment that mimics the actual testing experience as closely as possible. Find a quiet space where you can work without interruptions, and set a timer to hold yourself accountable to the same time constraints you'll face on the Digital SAT®. As you work through each question, focus on applying the strategies you've learned, such as breaking down complex problems into smaller steps, eliminating incorrect answer choices, and double-checking your work.

If you find yourself struggling with a particular question or concept, don't hesitate to go back and review the relevant section of the guide. Use the practice exercises as an opportunity to pinpoint areas where you need to spend more time and attention. Keep track of the questions you answer incorrectly and make a note of the concepts or skills that gave you trouble. This will help you tailor your study plan to focus on the areas where you have the most room for improvement.

After completing each set of practice exercises, take the time to carefully review the explanations provided for each question. Even if you answered a question correctly, reading the explanation can help you confirm your understanding and expose you to alternative problem-solving approaches. For the questions you answered incorrectly, pay close attention to where you went wrong and what you can learn from your mistakes. Use this feedback to adjust your study strategies and focus your efforts on the concepts that are most challenging for you.

Taking Full-Length Practice Tests

In addition to the chapter-specific practice exercises, this study guide includes full-length practice tests that mirror the format and content of the actual Digital SAT®. These practice tests are a crucial component of your preparation, as they provide you with the most accurate representation of what you'll face on exam day.

Aim to take at least two full-length practice tests during your study journey, ideally spacing them out to allow time for targeted practice and improvement between each test. Treat each practice test as if it were the real exam, following all the rules and time constraints. This will help you build stamina, manage stress, and identify any areas where you need to focus your study efforts.

After completing each practice test, carefully review your results. Analyze your performance in each section, noting your strengths and weaknesses. Use this information to adjust your study plan, dedicating more time to the areas where you struggled and reinforcing your understanding of the topics you've mastered.

Supplementing Your Study

While this study guide provides a comprehensive foundation for your Digital SAT® preparation, it's important to supplement your learning with additional resources. The College Board, which administers the SAT®, offers a wealth of official practice materials, including full-length tests and interactive tools. Incorporating these resources into your study plan will expose you to a wider range of questions and help you become more familiar with the digital testing interface.

In addition to official resources, consider exploring other reputable study materials, such as review books, online courses, and tutoring services. These resources can provide alternative explanations, additional practice questions, and personalized guidance to help you reach your goals.

Adapting to the Digital Format

One of the unique challenges of the Digital SAT® is adapting to the digital testing environment. While the content and question types are similar to the paper-based SAT®, the digital format presents its own set of considerations.

To prepare for the digital testing experience, familiarize yourself with the interface and tools available during the exam. The guide provides an overview of the digital format in Chapter 2, including how to navigate the test, use the built-in tools, and manage your time effectively. Practice using these features during your study sessions to become more comfortable with the digital environment.

It's also essential to consider the technical aspects of digital testing, such as ensuring a stable internet connection and having a reliable testing device. Make sure to review the technical requirements for the Digital SAT® and plan accordingly to minimize any potential issues on test day.

Developing a Positive Mindset

In addition to the practical strategies and techniques covered in this guide, cultivating a positive mindset is crucial for success on the Digital SAT®. Test anxiety and self-doubt can significantly impact your performance, even if you've thoroughly prepared.

Throughout your study journey, focus on building confidence in your abilities. Celebrate your progress and achievements, no matter how small they may seem. Remember that the Digital SAT® is just one step in your academic journey, and your scores do not define your worth or potential.

As you approach test day, prioritize self-care and stress management. Engage in activities that help you relax and recharge, such as exercise, meditation, or spending time with loved ones. Ensure that you're getting enough sleep, eating well, and staying hydrated to support your physical and mental well-being.

PART I

UNDERSTANDING THE DIGITAL SAT®

CHAPTER 1
THE DIGITAL SAT® EXPLAINED

The SAT® test is changing. Now, instead of using paper, you'll use a tablet to read and answer questions. This might make some people worried, but it's actually a good thing. It helps students get ready for tests that use computers, which are becoming more common in college and jobs. But, it's important to get ready for these changes before you take the test.

OVERVIEW OF THE DIGITAL SAT®

After nearly a century assessing students using paper booklets, the SAT® exam transitioned to a fully online digital format in 2023. While core assessed skills remain unchanged, this evolution necessitated adjustments to testing logistics and procedures. A thorough understanding of these changes empowers students with the knowledge to confidently focus on displaying their skills rather than grappling with technological intricacies.

The Digital Testing Experience

On the day of the exam, students go to special places for the test. They show their ID on a computer. Then they get a tablet with special test software. They also get things like calculators and headphones that are allowed. Before they start the timed parts of the test, they do practice questions to understand how the test works. They can use the tools on the tablet to help them. During the test, they can't connect to the internet so they don't get distracted or cheat. Teachers watch them to make sure they follow the rules, but they can't help with the questions or how to use the tools.

Digital Question Formats

To make the digital test easier to use, we changed how some questions look. Instead of filling in bubbles with a pencil, students now pick answers from a list that drops down. Some questions let students move things around on the screen. Also, instead of seeing a whole page of questions at once, students see one question at a time. This helps them concentrate better. They can also go back to earlier questions before the time for that section is up.

Accessibility by Design

The digital platform makes it easier for all students to take the test. Here are some ways it helps:

- Students can change the size of the words on the screen.
- They can choose to have the questions read aloud in English or Spanish.
- They can zoom in and out on the screen.
- They get math help with digital reference sheets and can use basic calculators.
- In the testing room, students sit at their own tables that are far apart from each other.
- Teachers watch to make sure everyone follows the rules, but they can't help with the questions.
- Students get breaks after big parts of the test, and also after smaller parts of the math test to rest their eyes.
- Scores are calculated based on right, wrong, and missed answers, and then changed to a 1600-point scale.
- Two weeks after the test, students get a digital report that shows how they did on different types of questions. This helps them know what to study next time.

DIFFERENCES BETWEEN DIGITAL AND PAPER-BASED SAT®

Format and Interface

One of the most apparent differences between the digital and paper SAT® is the format and interface.

The paper SAT® is administered in a physical test booklet that students read and fill out with pencil. Students must carefully bubble in their answers on a separate answer sheet. The test booklet contains all reading passages and questions.

The digital SAT® is taken entirely on a computer or tablet device. The exam interface has built-in tools like a timer, highlighter, and line reader. Students click or tap to select their answers. Reading passages appear on the left side of the screen with questions on the right. Students can easily scroll or navigate between passages and questions. Approx. 80% of questions are multiple choice, with the remaining 20% being technology-enhanced numeric entry or student-produced response questions.

While the digital format may be more familiar and comfortable for many students accustomed to working on computers, the change could be an adjustment for those more used to taking exams on paper. Practicing with the digital exam's interface and tools beforehand will help students feel prepared.

Adaptivity

A key feature of the digital SAT® is that it is section-level adaptive, meaning the difficulty of the second Math module and the Reading & Writing section adapts based on the student's performance on the previous portion.

The paper exam contains a fixed set of questions with a consistent difficulty level. Every student who takes a particular test administration sees the same questions in the same order regardless of their performance.

On the digital SAT®, every student starts with a module containing questions of medium difficulty. The subsequent Math module and Reading & Writing section then adapt to contain a harder or easier set of questions based on performance on the previous portion.

This adaptivity allows the digital SAT® to zero in on the student's ability level and produce a more precise score. High-performing students will be appropriately challenged while the exam won't become overwhelming for those who start struggling. At the same time, starting strong is extra important on the digital SAT® to ensure the later modules provide an opportunity to showcase one's maximum potential.

Timing Tools

The digital SAT® includes several built-in timing tools to help students pace themselves. Unlike the paper exam, where test-takers must use a watch or clock and rely on periodic warnings from proctors, the digital version provides an on-screen countdown timer. This timer, which can be hidden if distracting, displays the time remaining in each section. Additionally, the interface shows a progress bar indicating the portion of the section completed so far.

These tools can help reduce stress for many students, allowing them to focus more on the passage and questions rather than frequently checking a watch. However, some may find the countdown timer and progress bar anxiety-inducing. In such cases, students can hide the timer and practice using the digital test's timing tools to determine their preferred approach. Despite these tools, creating a pacing plan based on the number of questions and time per section remains valuable.

Test Timing

Component	Time Allotted (minutes)	Number of Questions/Tasks
Reading and Writing	64 (two 32-minute modules)	54
Math	70 (two 35-minute modules)	44
Total	134	98

Having a clear understanding of the timing for each section helps students develop an effective pacing strategy.

Navigation and Flagging

The digital SAT® offers some convenient navigation and answer-flagging capabilities.

On the paper exam, students must physically flip pages in the test booklet to move between passages and questions. If they want to skip a question and return to it later, they must note the question number on scratch paper as their answer sheet will be collected separately.

The digital SAT®'s navigation tools allow students to easily scroll or click to jump between passages and questions. A dropdown menu provides one-click access to any question. Students can digitally flag questions to revisit later. At the end of each section, they are automatically directed to answer any unflagged questions before moving on.

The ability to quickly navigate and flag questions on the digital SAT® may make it easier for students to implement skipping strategies and avoid getting stuck. Being automatically prompted to address skipped questions prevents accidentally leaving any blank.

However, digital test-takers must still be disciplined about pacing and avoiding distraction. Aimlessly clicking around the exam wastes precious time. Students should practice using the navigation tools effectively and having a strategic skipping plan.

Scratch Paper

Both SAT® formats allow students to use scratch paper, but the digital version has some specific guidelines.

Paper test-takers can use their test booklet or separate sheets of scratch paper to take notes, outline, solve math problems, etc. Scratch work is collected but not graded.

Digital test-takers receive separate scratch paper from the proctor. They may not use their own paper. Scratch paper is collected and destroyed after the exam to protect exam security since students testing across multiple time zones will see different questions. The interface also includes a digital notepad tool.

While students taking the digital SAT® can still use scratch paper to the same benefit as on the paper exam, it's important that they use only the official sheets provided on test day. They should get used to the routine of raising their hand to request additional scratch paper if needed during the exam.

The digital notepad may be convenient for jotting down quick thoughts, but most students will likely prefer physical paper for detailed work like annotation, outlining, and calculations. Practicing with the official scratch paper policy in mind will boost comfort on test day.

Highlighter and Line Focus Tools

The digital SAT® includes some tools designed to enhance focus and make annotation easier compared to the paper-based version.

Students taking the paper exam often underline or circle key parts of the passage and questions using their pencil. They must be careful to do so lightly so the text remains readable.

The digital SAT®'s interface includes a highlighter tool that students can use to highlight text within passages and questions. They can select from multiple colors. There is also a line focus tool that grays out surrounding text to help students zero in on one part of the passage at a time.

Tactile learners may feel that annotating with a physical pencil helps them engage with the content better than digital tools. But for many students, the ability to cleanly highlight text (and erase highlights if needed) without obscuring the passage will be an advantage of the digital SAT®.

The line focus tool provides an easy way to combat distraction and hone in on essential information. Students who struggle with extended screen reading may find this especially useful. Practicing with the highlighter and line focus tools during digital prep will help students optimize their usage on test day.

Calculator Policy

Another key difference between the paper and digital SAT® is the calculator policy.

The paper SAT® allows test-takers to bring their own approved calculator to use on one of the Math sections. Acceptable models include most common graphing and scientific calculators. Students are responsible for ensuring their calculator has sufficient battery/power.

The digital SAT® has an on-screen graphical calculator built into the interface for portions of the Math section designated as calculator allowed. Physical calculators are not permitted. The on-screen calculator has similar functions as the most common approved graphing calculators.

Not being able to use a familiar physical calculator and instead working with the built-in digital version will likely be an adjustment for many students. Those who are used to graphing calculator programs and shortcuts may need to spend some time learning the digital SAT® calculator's specific capabilities.

However, the on-screen calculator's inclusion of common graphing and scientific functions means most students will still have access to their essential math tools, and those without a physical graphing calculator are no longer at a disadvantage. Practicing with the exact on-screen calculator students will encounter reduces stress on test day.

Accommodations

Both the paper and digital SAT® offer accommodations for students with disabilities, but the digital version provides some additional options.

Students approved for accommodations on the paper SAT® may receive large-print test booklets, extra time, extended breaks, a scribe or reader, and other provisions as designated by College Board. Students must apply for accommodations well in advance of the test date.

The digital SAT® includes most of the same accommodations as the paper version, such as extended time, longer breaks, and screen readers. It additionally offers some enhanced accessibility features like ZoomText to enlarge the text and graphics, JAWS assistive technology, refreshable Braille, and a mouse-pointer indicator.

The streamlined accommodations request process for the digital SAT® may make it easier for students to access the supports they need. Students can practice on an assistive device or computer with accessibility features to simulate their digital testing experience.

However, as accommodations may modify the digital SAT®'s adaptive nature, students should confirm the specific format of their accommodated exam. Some may prefer accommodations on the paper test if a more predictable format increases their comfort level.

Question Formatting

Paper tests historically comprised printed booklets containing grids of multiple-choice bubbles alongside paragraph-length reading passages and written math expressions. Comparatively, the digital interface displays content sequentially across individual question screens, sometimes integrating interactive elements like drop-down menus necessitating careful selection via touch. Condensed formatting streamlines on-screen reading versus paper equivalents yet demands swift adaptation of response methods.

Scoring & Reporting

Raw scores still convert into the standard maximum 1600 scale depending on number of correct responses minus errors across equally-weighted Math, Reading and Writing sections. However, digital score reports arrive faster via online portals versus paper mailed statements and analyze performance longitudinally across successive digital SAT® administrations with greater insight through expanding dataset availability over time.

THE IMPORTANCE OF THE DIGITAL SAT®

Streamlining the Admissions Process

One of the primary advantages of the digital SAT® is its ability to streamline the college admissions process for both students and institutions.

With the paper-based SAT®, students often had to wait weeks to receive their scores, which could delay their college applications. The digital SAT® significantly reduces this turnaround time. Scores are typically available within days of taking the exam, allowing students to make informed decisions about where to apply much earlier in the process.

Many colleges are moving towards integrated digital application systems that allow students to submit their test scores, transcripts, and other materials all in one place. The digital SAT® aligns perfectly with this trend. Scores can be seamlessly incorporated into a student's online application profile, eliminating the need for separate score reports and reducing paperwork.

As more colleges adopt test-optional admissions policies, there is a growing need for alternative measures of student potential. The digital SAT® is designed to provide more robust data on a student's skills and knowledge that can be easily compared to other assessments like the ACT or state proficiency exams. This improved concordance helps admissions officers get a clearer picture of each applicant.

Expanding Educational Access

Another key benefit of the digital SAT® is its potential to expand access to higher education for students from all backgrounds.

The digital format allows the College Board to offer the SAT® on more dates throughout the year, including on weekdays. This flexibility makes it easier for students to find a time that works with their busy schedules and family obligations. Those who might have struggled to take the exam on a Saturday morning now have more options.

The digital SAT® interface includes several built-in accommodations like a highlighter tool, adjustable text size, and extended time. This means that students with disabilities or special needs may have an easier time accessing the appropriate accommodations without having to jump through as many hoops. The digital format also expands possibilities for accommodations as technology advances.

For students living in rural areas or without reliable transportation, getting to a physical testing location could be a major barrier. The digital SAT® can be administered at a student's own school or even at approved off-site locations with a proctor. This eliminates the need to travel long distances, reducing both cost and stress for test-takers.

Personalized Assessment Experience

The digital SAT® also offers opportunities for a more personalized assessment experience tailored to each student's unique needs and goals.

While the digital SAT® is not fully adaptive, it does incorporate some adaptive elements that adjust the difficulty of questions based on a student's performance. This helps to pinpoint a test-taker's ability level more precisely, providing colleges with a clearer picture of their academic strengths and weaknesses. Students are appropriately challenged without being overwhelmed.

The digital interface allows for more interactive question types beyond traditional multiple-choice. Students may be asked to drag and drop answer choices, highlight evidence in a passage, or manipulate graphs and charts. These question formats more closely mirror the types of tasks students will encounter in college courses and provide a better assessment of real-world skills.

One advantage of the digital format is the ability to provide students with instant feedback on their performance. Immediately after the exam, test-takers can see which questions they answered correctly and where they struggled. The College Board partners with online study platforms like Khan Academy to create personalized practice plans based on these results, helping students to target their prep more effectively.

Aligning with Workforce Readiness

In today's rapidly evolving economy, the skills needed for success in the workforce are changing. The digital SAT® is designed to assess not only academic knowledge but also the critical thinking, problem-solving, and technological skills that are in high demand.

The digital SAT® places a greater emphasis on data analysis and interpretation than the paper-based version. Students are asked to read and understand graphs, tables, and charts across all sections of the exam. This skill is increasingly important in fields like business, healthcare, and engineering where data-driven decision making is key.

The digital test interface allows for more scenario-based questions that give students a taste of real-world situations. For example, a reading passage might be presented as an email exchange between colleagues or a science question could describe a lab experiment. These questions assess how well students can apply their knowledge to solve practical problems.

By moving the SAT® online, the College Board is signaling the importance of digital literacy for college and career success. The exam's format aligns with the technological fluency students will need in higher education and the workforce. Students must be comfortable navigating digital interfaces, utilizing online tools, and interpreting data visualizations.

Supporting Continuous Improvement

Finally, the move to a digital SAT® supports a culture of continuous improvement in education, using data to identify areas of strength and opportunities for growth.

With faster score reporting, teachers and schools can access student performance data more quickly. This allows them to adjust instruction in real-time to better support student learning. For example, if a large percentage of students struggle with a particular math concept on the SAT®, teachers can prioritize that topic in their lesson plans.

The digital SAT® provides a wealth of data that can be analyzed to identify equity gaps in education. By looking at performance patterns across demographics like race, income, and geography, educators can see where additional resources or interventions may be needed to level the playing field. This data can inform school and district-level decisions about curriculum, funding, and student support services.

With millions of students taking the digital SAT® each year, the College Board is amassing a large dataset on student performance. This anonymized data can be used to support research on effective teaching and learning practices. Insights from the SAT® can help drive innovation in areas like personalized learning, adaptive assessments, and predictive analytics for student success.

The transition to a digital SAT® represents a major milestone in the world of educational assessment. By embracing technology and adapting to the needs of 21st century learners, the College Board is positioning the SAT® as a valuable tool for expanding access, promoting equity, and driving continuous improvement in education.

The benefits of the digital SAT® are numerous. From streamlining the admissions process and expanding testing opportunities to providing a more personalized assessment experience, the digital format has the potential to break down barriers and empower students from all backgrounds to pursue their college aspirations.

Moreover, by aligning with the skills and competencies needed for success in the modern workforce, the digital SAT® is helping to bridge the gap between high school and the demands of higher education and career. As students navigate an increasingly technological world, the ability to think critically, analyze data, and solve complex problems in a digital environment will be essential.

Of course, the transition to a digital SAT® is not without its challenges. Schools and students will need to ensure access to reliable technology and internet connectivity. Educators will need training and support to interpret and act on the wealth of data provided by the digital format. And as with any major change, there may be growing pains as students, parents, and colleges adapt to the new system.

Yet despite these challenges, the potential benefits of the digital SAT® far outweigh the risks. By embracing this change and working together to support its successful implementation, we have the opportunity to create a more equitable, effective, and forward-thinking educational landscape that truly prepares students for the challenges and opportunities of the 21st century.

SUBMIT A REVIEW

Did these pages help, inspire, or bring you value in any way? If so, we'd love to hear your thoughts through an honest review on Amazon. Your feedback is incredibly valuable to us!

It's very simple and only takes a few minutes:

1. Go to the "My Orders" page on Amazon and search the book.
2. Select "Write a product review".
3. Select a Star Rating.
4. Optionally, add text, photos, or videos and select Submit.

CHAPTER 2
NAVIGATING THE DIGITAL FORMAT

This chapter dives into making the most out of the online SAT®. It starts by explaining the tools and features of the digital test and advises students to practice with them ahead of time. Understanding the adaptive model, where question difficulty adjusts based on responses, can help students pace themselves better. The guide also covers dealing with common distractions like internet problems and eye strain. With fewer distractions from proctors, it's important for students to stay focused. The chapter wraps up by giving a structured plan for practicing in a way that simulates real test conditions.

By mastering the digital interface through consistent practice, students can feel more confident when taking the actual exam.

FAMILIARIZING YOURSELF WITH THE DIGITAL INTERFACE

Logging into Your Online Test

To ensure a smooth testing experience, it's essential to familiarize yourself with the login process and necessary preparations well before test day. The first step is to download the Bluebook exam app on the device you plan to use during the exam. If you're using a school-managed device, this step may be completed for you. Once the app is installed, log in using your College Board account credentials and complete the exam setup. During this process, Bluebook will load your specific exam onto your device and generate a unique admission ticket. It's crucial to print your admission ticket or email it to yourself, as you'll need to present it to the proctor on test day.

To familiarize yourself with the Digital SAT® interface and question types, take advantage of the "Practice and Prepare" section on the Bluebook application homepage. Here, you can access test previews and full-length practice tests, which will help you become more comfortable with the digital format and assess your readiness for the actual exam.

What to Bring on Test Day

On the day of your Digital SAT®, make sure to bring your fully charged testing device with the Bluebook app installed and exam setup completed. Don't forget your printed or digital admission ticket, as well as an approved photo ID, which you'll present to the proctor during check-in. To ensure your device remains powered throughout the exam, bring a power cord and/or a portable charger, as access to electrical outlets may be limited at the test center. Your device should be capable of holding a charge for at least 3–4 hours.

Bring a pencil or pen for scratch work, but keep in mind that scratch paper will be provided by the test center, so there's no need to bring your own. If you prefer to use your own calculator, make sure it's an approved model, although a graphing calculator is built into the Bluebook app. If you typically use an external mouse or keyboard (the latter is only allowed with tablets, not laptops), don't forget to bring those as well.

Taking the Digital SAT®

On test day, plan to arrive at your designated test center at least 15 minutes before your scheduled start time. Once you've located your assigned room, the proctor will check your admission ticket and photo ID before allowing you to enter. After taking your seat, connect your device to the provided Wi-Fi network, log into the Bluebook app, and complete the brief check-in process within the app.

Before the exam begins, your proctor will read a set of instructions, collect any prohibited items, and provide you with a unique start code. Enter this code into the Bluebook app to initiate your Digital SAT® exam. The test consists of two main sections: Reading and Writing, and Math. Each section is further divided into two separately timed modules. You can navigate freely between questions within a module and review your answers until the allotted time for that module expires.

You'll have a break between the two main sections. During this time, carefully follow all instructions displayed on the Bluebook break page to ensure a smooth transition to the next section. Once you've completed the entire exam, the Bluebook app will automatically submit your answers. It's crucial that you do not close your device until you see the "Congratulations!" screen, confirming that your submission was successful. In the event that your submission fails for any reason, the app will provide instructions on how to complete the submission process.

Interface

The Digital SAT® exam interface is designed to provide a user-friendly and intuitive testing experience for students. Understanding the features and layout of the interface is crucial for navigating the exam efficiently and maintaining focus on the tasks at hand. Let's explore the key components of the Digital SAT® interface.

Test Navigation

The Digital SAT®'s navigation bar is a critical tool for efficiently moving through the exam and managing your time effectively. Located at the bottom of the screen, the navigation bar displays the question numbers for the current section, with your current question highlighted for easy reference. To move between questions, simply click on the desired question number. This allows you to quickly jump to specific questions, skip questions that you want to return to later, or review your answers before submitting the section.

In addition to question numbers, the navigation bar may include other useful features. For example, you may see options to flag questions that you want to revisit, which can be particularly helpful if you're unsure of an answer or want to double-check your work. The navigation bar may also provide quick access to tools like the calculator or reference sheet, depending on the section and question type.

Answer Selection

When it comes to answering questions on the Digital SAT®, the interface is designed to be intuitive and user-friendly. For multiple-choice questions, which make up the majority of the exam, you'll see a list of answer options displayed directly beneath the question stem. To select your answer, simply click on the bubble or circle next to your chosen option. The interface will typically highlight your selection, making it easy to confirm your answer at a glance. If you change your mind or realize you've made a mistake, you can easily update your answer by clicking on a different option.

For grid-in questions, which appear in the Math section, you'll need to enter your answer using the digital keypad provided on the screen. The keypad includes numbers, a decimal point, and a negative sign, allowing you to enter a wide range of answers. When entering your answer, be sure to pay attention to the question's instructions and any specific formatting requirements. For example, some questions may ask for your answer in the form of a fraction or a decimal rounded to a certain number of places.

Timer and Progress Indicator

Effective time management is essential for success on the Digital SAT®, and the exam's interface includes several tools to help you stay on track. One of the most important of these tools is the timer, which displays the remaining time for the current section. The timer is typically located in a prominent position on the screen, such as in the corner or in the navigation bar, making it easy to glance at throughout the section. By keeping an eye on the timer, you can pace yourself appropriately and ensure that you have enough time to complete all the questions.

In addition to the timer, the Digital SAT® interface may include a progress indicator that shows your current position within the section. This indicator typically takes the form of a bar or a fraction, displaying the number of questions you've completed out of the total number of questions in the section. The progress indicator can be a valuable tool for gauging your pace and adjusting your strategy as needed. For example, if you notice that you're falling behind your desired pace, you may need to speed up or be more selective about which questions you spend the most time on.

Customizing Accessibility Preferences

During the exam, students can adjust settings like text size or hiding answered questions to help them perform better. These options are available in the sidebar and can make a big difference in how comfortable students feel. Unlike with paper tests, digital exams can offer more personalized accommodations. It's important for students to take time during practice sessions to figure out what settings work best for them and make notes so they can use them during the actual test. Being able to access these personalized supports comfortably shows what students are really capable of.

Question Styles

The Digital SAT® incorporates a variety of question styles to assess your knowledge and skills across different subjects. Familiarizing yourself with these question formats is essential for success on the exam, as each type requires a specific approach and strategy. Let's take a closer look at some of the most common question styles you'll encounter on the Digital SAT®.

Multiple-Choice Questions

Multiple-choice questions are a staple of the Digital SAT® and appear in all sections of the exam. These questions present a stem (the question or prompt) followed by four or five answer options. Your task is to select the best answer based on the information provided in the question. To tackle multiple-choice questions effectively, start by reading the stem carefully and identifying the key information. Then, consider each answer choice in turn, eliminating those that are clearly incorrect or irrelevant. If you're unsure of the correct answer, use the process of elimination to narrow down your options and make an educated guess.

Evidence-Based Questions

Evidence-based questions are a unique feature of the Digital SAT® Reading section. These questions come in pairs, with the first question asking about the content of the passage and the second question asking you to select the evidence from the passage that best supports your answer to the first question. To approach evidence-based questions, start by answering the first question based on your understanding of the passage. Then, look back at the passage to find the specific evidence that supports your answer. Be sure to read the lines referenced in each answer choice carefully to determine which one most directly supports your response to the first question.

Grid-In Questions

Grid-in questions, also known as student-produced response questions, appear in the Math section of the Digital SAT®. Unlike multiple-choice questions, grid-in questions do not provide a list of answer choices. Instead, you'll need to solve the problem and enter your answer into a grid on the screen. Grid-in questions may require you to enter a numerical answer, a fraction, or a decimal. When answering grid-in questions, be sure to read the instructions carefully and double-check your work before entering your answer. Keep in mind that there may be multiple correct ways to enter your answer, so don't worry if your response doesn't match the exact formatting of the sample answers provided.

Passage-Based Questions

Passage-based questions are common in the Reading and Writing and Language sections of the Digital SAT®. These questions assess your ability to read and interpret written passages, as well as your understanding of grammar, usage, and style. To approach passage-based questions, start by reading the passage carefully and actively, taking notes on key ideas and details. Then, read each question and refer back to the passage to find the information needed to answer it. Be sure to consider the context of the passage as a whole when selecting your answer, rather than relying on isolated phrases or sentences.

Data Analysis Questions

Data analysis questions appear in the Math section of the Digital SAT® and assess your ability to interpret and manipulate data presented in tables, graphs, and charts. These questions may ask you to calculate values, compare quantities, or draw conclusions based on the data provided. To approach data analysis questions, start by carefully examining the data and identifying the key information needed to answer the question. Then, use your knowledge of mathematical concepts and problem-solving strategies to determine the correct answer. Be sure to pay attention to the units and scales used in the data, and double-check your calculations before selecting your answer.

ADAPTIVE TESTING

Unlike older standardized tests with fixed scales, Computer-Adaptive Testing (CAT) adapts to each student's performance. If a student answers correctly, the next question becomes more challenging. If they answer incorrectly, the difficulty decreases momentarily to ensure understanding before gradually increasing again. This dynamic process accurately assesses each student's abilities rather than ranking them against each other broadly. Personalization helps students stay engaged within their individual zones of development.

Maximizing Student-Centered Support

The adaptive approach not only reduces frustration but also allows students to demonstrate their skills more accurately through customized curriculums. By analyzing performance trends across tasks of varying difficulty levels, educators gain detailed insights beyond just averages, enabling personalized support. Students can take control of their pacing, finishing sections early once they've met proficiency standards. This autonomy fosters intrinsic motivation, which is crucial for long-term success.

Comprehensive Algorithmic Processes

The computer-graded adaptive sections consist of about 15 sets of questions, each drawing from a large digital pool of items. These sections last for 100 minutes. Behind the smooth operation of the system are statistical analyses of responses, which are compared against challenge thresholds established from years of pilot data. Using probabilistic programming, the system considers past examinee data, current skills demonstrated, and the attributes of the next question to select the most suitable items in sequence, tailored to the emerging ability estimates with each answer submitted.

Individualized Outcomes

After finishing the test, candidates get detailed reports on their personalized test experiences. These reports show how they performed across different levels of difficulty, highlighting strengths and areas for improvement. This targeted feedback goes beyond traditional summaries, helping candidates focus their practice more effectively. By strategically using these insights, candidates can address weaknesses even if they didn't score below average overall.

Leveraging Adaptive Opportunities

By getting to know the sophisticated CAT mechanisms used in standardized tests, students can better showcase their knowledge. Understanding how personalized questions are selected gives students more control over their pacing and timing for each section. Detailed post-exam diagnostics provide insights into personalized learning priorities by showing how abilities changed throughout the test. Adaptive testing embodies a student-focused approach that maximizes potential through customization.

TIPS FOR MANAGING THE DIGITAL TEST ENVIRONMENT

With less proctor oversight in digital testing, self-discipline becomes crucial. However, building this stamina requires accurately replicating test pressures. Set aside uninterrupted blocks of time that match section timings to avoid distractions from devices or the internet, allowing up to fifteen minutes to regain focus after a distraction. For better isolation, consider using public workspaces or browser extensions that block unrelated web usage temporarily. By practicing in conditions that mimic the real test environment, you can build mental fortitude and become more comfortable with engaging assessments, authentically representing your competence online.

Overcome Connectivity Issues Proactively

Digital tests offer accessibility benefits, but technical issues are inevitable on any platform. To prepare, create a backup plan that includes alternative devices or postponing the test if needed. Coordinate with technical support personnel to troubleshoot any issues beforehand and avoid last-minute disruptions. Utilize official practice exams to identify individual device strengths and weaknesses in a controlled environment. Proactively addressing any issues helps alleviate pressure from unexpected problems on test day.

Experiment with Built-In Accommodations Freely

There are universal tools available to enhance focus, like text magnification, audio playback, or answer masking. However, finding the best settings for you requires extensive trial and error during multiple full-length practice exams that replicate real testing conditions. Record the refined settings that work best for you so you can apply them directly during the actual test. Additionally, discuss any pre-approved specialized needs upfront to ensure that the necessary paperwork is processed smoothly and you receive the support you require. Being prepared ensures that you're focusing on your skills rather than trying to navigate unfamiliar interfaces under time constraints during the test.

Establish an Ideal Private Testing Space

Creating an ergonomic, distraction-free area for dedicated practice that mirrors official testing centers is essential. Consider conducting expedited WiFi tests to ensure stable internet connection. Arrange lighting ergonomically for prolonged screen time, and set up seating and equipment in a comfortable configuration. Pay attention to ambient noises and other variables that could impact concentration. Reserve this optimized space exclusively for focused practice sessions that authentically replicate testing conditions, including timings and breaks between sections. By conditioning yourself in a familiar, controlled environment, you can enhance concentration and consistently represent your abilities online.

Leverage Community Support Networks

Collaborating with accountability partners is often more effective than isolated test preparation. Consider joining study groups where members use the same digital platforms to share experiences and strategize on how to optimize settings together. Seek out mentors, tutors, counseling professionals, disability service coordinators, and others who are invested in your academic success. Their guidance can help reinforce individualized study routines, preparing you mentally and technically for the test by leveraging all available resources. Building a well-rounded support network demonstrates dedication to maximizing opportunities accessed through assessments.

Monitoring Personal Wellness Holistically

In addition to academic preparation, it's crucial to monitor overall wellness, as it can impact performance under pressure. Prioritize getting enough sleep, eating nutritious food, exercising regularly, engaging socially, and managing stress. With digital exams, it's important to avoid sedentary isolation, which can affect memory retention and focused persistence negatively. By maintaining a balanced lifestyle that mirrors the expectations of independent learning, you can condition yourself to feel empowered and authentically represent your full capacities online.

✦ ✦ ✦ ✦ ✦

SUBMIT A REVIEW

Did these pages help, inspire, or bring you value in any way? If so, we'd love to hear your thoughts through an honest review on Amazon. Your feedback is incredibly valuable to us!

It's very simple and only takes a few minutes:

1. Go to the "My Orders" page on Amazon and search the book.
2. Select "Write a product review".
3. Select a Star Rating.
4. Optionally, add text, photos, or videos and select Submit.

DISCLAIMER

The questions and content presented in this book have been meticulously developed by the author using a variety of reputable educational resources, including Digital SAT® practice materials. These materials have been adapted, modified, and created to align with the educational objectives of this study guide.

It is crucial to understand that while the utmost care has been taken to ensure the quality and accuracy of the questions and content, they are not endorsed by the College Board, the organization responsible for the Digital SAT® examination. Furthermore, the questions and content in this study guide may not be representative of actual Digital SAT® exam questions, and no assurances are made regarding their similarity to questions that may appear on the official Digital SAT® exam.

Moreover, any resemblance between the questions and content in this study guide and those found on official Digital SAT® exams is entirely coincidental. The primary purpose of this study guide is to provide students with comprehensive practice and instruction to support their preparation for the Digital SAT® exam.

By utilizing this study guide, readers acknowledge and understand that the questions and content are for educational purposes only and are not intended to replicate the exact content of the Digital SAT® exam. The author and publisher assume no responsibility for any consequences arising from the use or misuse of the materials presented herein.

PART II
EVIDENCE-BASED READING AND WRITING

CHAPTER 3
READING COMPREHENSION STRATEGIES

This chapter focuses on mastering the analytical skills needed for the Evidence-Based Reading and Writing section of the exam. It starts by discussing how to actively engage with different types of passages through careful reading. Techniques for understanding vocabulary in context, identifying key details and themes, and recognizing implicit meanings are covered. Next, it explores various question formats designed to assess higher-order thinking skills. Strategies for systematically arriving at well-supported answers by referring back to evidence from the passage are explained. The chapter includes hands-on exercises where readers can apply these reading comprehension strategies to authentic reading excerpts similar to those on the SAT®. Detailed explanations of answers help reinforce mastery of the literacy skills assessed by the exam. Students gain insights into their strengths and areas for improvement, allowing them to focus their practice effectively.

UNDERSTANDING AND ANALYZING PASSAGES

Mastering the art of understanding and analyzing passages is a critical skill for success on the SAT®. This guide provides a comprehensive set of strategies to help you effectively showcase your higher-order thinking abilities. By consistently practicing these techniques, you can approach the exam with confidence and demonstrate your proficiency in reading comprehension.

When tackling a passage, begin by actively reading the text, focusing on key details, main ideas, and the overall structure. Pay attention to the author's purpose, tone, and perspective, as these elements often provide valuable insights into the deeper meaning of the passage. As you read, engage with the text by asking yourself questions, making predictions, and connecting the information to your prior knowledge.

Narrative Passages

Narrative passages on the SAT® often take the form of short stories or excerpts from novels. These texts utilize a range of literary devices to convey themes, messages, and insights that go beyond the surface-level plot. To effectively understand and analyze narrative passages, you must engage with the text on a deeper level, considering elements such as characterization, setting, and symbolism.

As you read a narrative passage, actively visualize the scenes, characters, and environments described by the author. Pay attention to sensory details, such as sights, sounds, and textures, which can help bring the story to life in your mind. By immersing yourself in the world of the narrative, you'll be better equipped to understand the relationships between characters, the significance of their actions, and the overall atmosphere of the piece.

One key aspect of analyzing narrative passages is identifying the point of view from which the story is told. Consider whether the narrator is a character within the story (first-person perspective) or an outside observer (third-person perspective). Assess the narrator's reliability and potential biases, as these can influence the way events and characters are portrayed.

As you read, also pay attention to the development of characters throughout the narrative. Note their personality traits, motivations, and relationships with other characters. Consider how their actions, thoughts, and dialogue contribute to the overall themes and messages of the story. Look for patterns or changes in their behavior that may signal growth, conflict, or revelation.

Another important element to consider when analyzing narrative passages is the use of symbolism. Authors often employ objects, colors, or events as symbols to represent abstract ideas or themes. For example, a stormy sea might symbolize emotional turmoil, while a character's journey could represent a quest for self-discovery. Identify potential symbols in the passage and consider their significance in relation to the larger themes of the narrative.

Examine the structure and pacing of the narrative. Consider how the author builds tension, reveals information, and resolves conflicts. Pay attention to the use of flashbacks, foreshadowing, and other narrative techniques that can contribute to the overall impact of the story.

History/Social Studies Passages

History and social studies passages on the SAT® often present information from primary or secondary sources, such as historical documents, speeches, or scholarly articles. These texts aim to discuss topics, events, and time periods objectively, synthesizing research from credible sources. To effectively understand and analyze these passages, you must be able to identify key information, recognize relationships between concepts, and evaluate the author's arguments.

As you read a history or social studies passage, pay attention to the main idea or thesis statement, which is often presented in the introduction. This will give you a sense of the overall purpose and focus of the text. Then, as you read through the body paragraphs, note the supporting details, examples, and evidence that the author uses to develop their argument.

One effective strategy for understanding the structure of a history or social studies passage is to create a brief outline or summary of the main points. This can help you keep track of the key ideas and see how they relate to one another. Additionally, pay attention to any transitions or connections between paragraphs, as these often signal important shifts in the author's argument or the introduction of new concepts.

When analyzing a history or social studies passage, it's crucial to consider the historical context in which the events or ideas discussed take place. Think about the social, political, and economic factors that may have influenced the author's perspective or the development of the concepts presented. By situating the passage within its broader historical framework, you'll be better equipped to understand the significance of the information provided.

As you read, also pay attention to any specific individuals, groups, or organizations mentioned in the passage. Consider their roles, actions, and impact on the events or ideas discussed. Look for any patterns or trends that emerge across different historical periods or social contexts, as these can provide valuable insights into the larger themes or issues at play.

Another important aspect of analyzing history and social studies passages is evaluating the author's use of sources and evidence. Consider the credibility and reliability of the information presented, and look for any potential biases or limitations in the author's perspective. Assess the strength of the arguments made and the extent to which the evidence supports the main points of the passage.

Science Passages

Science passages on the SAT® often present findings from empirical research, such as controlled experiments or studies. These texts aim to communicate scientific information accurately and objectively, discussing hypotheses, methodologies, results, and conclusions. To effectively understand and analyze science passages, you must be able to interpret data, evaluate evidence, and understand the implications of the research presented.

As you read a science passage, begin by identifying the main research question or hypothesis being investigated. This will help you understand the overall purpose and focus of the study. Then, pay close attention to the methodology section, which describes how the experiment or study was conducted. Note details such as the sample size, variables measured, and any control groups used, as these factors can influence the reliability and validity of the results.

When analyzing the results section of a science passage, look for key findings and trends in the data. Pay attention to any graphs, charts, or tables that may be included, as these visual representations can often provide a clearer picture of the outcomes. Consider how the results relate to the initial hypothesis and whether they support or refute the researcher's predictions.

Dual Passages

Dual passages on the SAT® present two texts that discuss a similar topic or theme from different perspectives. These passages provide an opportunity for you to demonstrate your ability to analyze and synthesize information from multiple sources, compare and contrast viewpoints, and evaluate the strengths and weaknesses of each author's arguments. To effectively understand and analyze dual passages, you must be able to identify the main ideas and key details in each text, recognize the relationship between the passages, and assess the implications of their similarities and differences.

When approaching dual passages, start by reading each text separately, focusing on the main ideas, supporting details, and overall perspective presented. As you read, make brief notes or annotations to help you keep track of the key points and distinguish between the two passages. Pay attention to the authors' tones, styles, and use of evidence, as these elements can provide valuable insights into their individual perspectives.

After reading both passages, take a moment to reflect on their relationship to one another. Consider whether the texts present opposing viewpoints, complementary ideas, or a mix of both. Look for any explicit references or allusions that one passage makes to the other, as these can help you understand the dialogue between the two texts.

When comparing and contrasting the passages, focus on the specific aspects of the topic that each author emphasizes or downplays. Consider how their arguments differ in terms of the evidence they present, the assumptions they make, and the conclusions they draw. Assess the strengths and limitations of each perspective, and evaluate which author presents a more convincing or well-supported argument.

ANSWERING COMPREHENSION QUESTIONS ACCURATELY

To excel on the SAT®, it's essential to develop a strong approach for answering comprehension questions accurately. These questions test your ability to understand and analyze the information presented in the passages, and they often require you to draw inferences, make connections, and evaluate arguments. By mastering a few key strategies, you can improve your accuracy and efficiency in tackling comprehension questions.

First, make sure you have a thorough understanding of the passage before attempting to answer any questions. Take the time to read the text carefully, focusing on the main ideas, supporting details, and overall structure. As you read, actively engage with the material by asking yourself questions, making predictions, and connecting the information to your prior knowledge. This deep level of engagement will help you better retain and recall the key points when answering questions.

When you encounter a comprehension question, start by identifying the type of information being asked for. Some questions may require you to locate specific details from the passage, while others may ask you to infer meaning, analyze tone, or evaluate an argument. Understanding the nature of the question can help you focus your attention on the most relevant aspects of the text.

Next, refer back to the passage to find the information needed to answer the question. Use keywords from the question to guide your search, and pay attention to the context surrounding the relevant details. If the question asks about a specific line or paragraph, make sure to read a few sentences before and after the referenced text to gain a fuller understanding of the context.

When considering answer choices, use the process of elimination to rule out options that are clearly incorrect or irrelevant. Focus on the specific wording of each choice, and compare it to the information presented in the passage. Be cautious of answers that are only partially correct or that make assumptions not supported by the text. The correct answer should be fully consistent with the information provided and should directly address the question being asked.

In some cases, you may need to make inferences or draw conclusions based on the information presented in the passage. When doing so, be sure to base your reasoning on the evidence provided, rather than relying on outside knowledge or personal opinions. Consider the implications of the passage as a whole, and look for clues that support your inferences.

If you're unsure about an answer, try to eliminate as many choices as possible and then make an educated guess from the remaining options. It's important to answer every question, as there is no penalty for incorrect answers on the SAT®. However, if you find yourself spending too much time on a particularly challenging question, it may be wise to make a quick guess and move on to the next one, returning to the difficult question later if time allows.

PRACTICE EXERCISES

Exercise 1

QUESTION 1:

In recent years, the destruction of rainforests has garnered significant attention. These vital ecosystems, home to countless species, are being cleared at alarming rates. Conservationists argue that preserving these habitats is essential not only for biodiversity but also for the health of our planet. They stress the importance of protecting natural environments to ensure ecological balance and the survival of various species.

What is the main theme of the passage? A) The impact of industrialization on society

    B) The importance of preserving natural habitats
    C) The development of modern transportation
    D) The challenges faced by early settlers

The correct answer is B - the importance of preserving natural habitats. The passage discusses the effects of human activity on natural environments and emphasizes the need for conservation efforts to protect these areas.

QUESTION 2:

Renewable energy, such as solar and wind power, is increasingly seen as a solution to the world's energy crisis. These sources are sustainable and have a lower environmental impact compared to fossil fuels. Proponents of renewable energy believe it can significantly reduce our dependence on non-renewable resources and help combat climate change. They argue that with technological advancements, renewable energy can meet global energy needs efficiently.

Which statement best summarizes the author's argument about renewable energy? A) Renewable energy sources are unreliable and costly.

    B) Renewable energy has the potential to meet global energy needs.
    C) Fossil fuels are more efficient than renewable energy sources.
    D) Renewable energy development has been largely unsuccessful.

The correct answer is B - renewable energy has the potential to meet global energy needs. The passage highlights the advantages and potential of renewable energy sources in addressing global energy demands.

QUESTION 3:

The integration of technology in education has revolutionized the learning process. Interactive tools and digital platforms have made education more accessible and engaging. Teachers can use multimedia resources to enhance lessons, and students can benefit from personalized learning experiences. This technological shift supports a modern educational environment that prepares students for the future.

How does the author describe the relationship between technology and education in the passage? A) Technology hinders the learning process.

B) Technology is an unnecessary addition to education.
C) Technology enhances and supports modern education.
D) Technology has no significant impact on education.

The correct answer is C - technology enhances and supports modern education. The passage elaborates on how technological advancements have improved educational methods and accessibility.

QUESTION 4:

A recent study conducted by leading scientists has shown a direct correlation between physical activity and mental health. The research found that regular exercise can significantly reduce symptoms of depression and anxiety. By highlighting this study, the author underscores the importance of physical activity as a crucial component of mental health care.

What is the author's purpose in mentioning a specific scientific study in the passage? A) To discredit the findings of the study

B) To provide evidence supporting the main argument
C) To illustrate a controversial viewpoint
D) To question the validity of scientific research

The correct answer is B - to provide evidence supporting the main argument. The passage uses the study to back up the author's claims and reinforce the overall thesis.

QUESTION 5:

The government's decision to overhaul the healthcare system aimed to make medical services more affordable. However, the abrupt implementation led to widespread confusion and dissatisfaction. Many citizens felt uncertain about their coverage, leading to a decline in public trust in the government's ability to manage healthcare effectively.

According to the passage, what was one major consequence of the policy change discussed? A) Increased economic stability

B) Decline in public trust
C) Expansion of social services
D) Growth in employment opportunities

The correct answer is B - decline in public trust. The passage explains how the policy change led to widespread skepticism and reduced confidence among the public.

QUESTION 6:

Throughout history, art has been a profound expression of cultural values. From ancient cave paintings to contemporary installations, art reflects the beliefs, traditions, and societal norms of the times. It serves as a cultural mirror, offering insights into the human experience and the evolution of civilization.

What does the author suggest about the role of art in society? A) Art is solely for entertainment.

   B) Art is a reflection of cultural values.
   C) Art is a luxury that few can afford.
   D) Art is irrelevant in modern times.

The correct answer is B - art is a reflection of cultural values. The passage discusses how art serves as a mirror to societal norms, beliefs, and historical contexts.

QUESTION 7:

The author discusses the rising global temperatures and their impact on weather patterns, wildlife, and human life. They emphasize the urgent need for action to mitigate these effects and highlight the potential consequences of inaction. The author's tone conveys a deep concern for the future, advocating for sustainable practices to combat climate change.

What can be inferred about the author's perspective on climate change? A) The author is skeptical about the existence of climate change.

   B) The author believes climate change is a natural phenomenon.
   C) The author is concerned about the impacts of climate change.
   D) The author thinks climate change is an exaggerated issue.

The correct answer is C - the author is concerned about the impacts of climate change. The passage conveys the author's worries regarding the consequences of climate change and advocates for proactive measures.

QUESTION 8:

As Sarah embarked on her solo journey across the country, she encountered numerous obstacles that tested her resilience. From navigating unfamiliar terrain to overcoming personal fears, each challenge contributed to her growth. Sarah's experiences transformed her, teaching her valuable lessons about strength and perseverance.

How does the passage characterize the protagonist's journey? A) As a series of fortunate events

B) As a struggle for personal growth
C) As an effortless adventure
D) As a mundane routine

The correct answer is B - as a struggle for personal growth. The passage describes the protagonist's challenges and the lessons learned throughout their journey, highlighting their development.

QUESTION 9:

Artificial intelligence (AI) is rapidly advancing, offering unprecedented opportunities in fields like healthcare, finance, and transportation. Experts believe that AI has the potential to revolutionize these industries by improving efficiency and accuracy. The future of AI looks promising, with continued innovations likely to enhance various aspects of our lives.

What does the author imply about the future of artificial intelligence? A) It will render human workers obsolete.

B) It will create more problems than it solves.
C) It holds great promise for various fields.
D) It is unlikely to advance further.

The correct answer is C - it holds great promise for various fields. The passage discusses the potential benefits and applications of artificial intelligence in diverse areas.

QUESTION 10:

Economic inequality has become a pressing issue in modern society. Studies reveal that the wealth gap between the richest and the poorest continues to widen. Statistical data shows significant disparities in income, access to education, and healthcare. This growing divide has sparked debates about the need for policies to address economic inequality and promote social justice.

What evidence does the author use to support their claim about economic inequality? A) Anecdotal stories from individuals

B) Statistical data and research studies
C) Personal opinions and beliefs
D) Historical events and timelines

The correct answer is B - statistical data and research studies. The passage provides empirical evidence and data to substantiate the author's argument regarding economic disparity.

Exercise 2

QUESTION 1:

The phenomenon of urbanization has transformed cities into bustling hubs of economic and social activity. However, this rapid growth often comes at a cost. Many cities struggle with overcrowding, pollution, and insufficient infrastructure. Urban planners emphasize the need for sustainable development practices to create livable cities that balance growth with environmental and social well-being.

What issue is highlighted as a consequence of urbanization in the passage?

A) Economic decline
B) Overcrowding and pollution
C) Decreased social interaction
D) Improved infrastructure

The correct answer is B - overcrowding and pollution. The passage discusses the challenges cities face due to rapid urbanization, including overcrowding and pollution.

QUESTION 2:

Recent advancements in biotechnology have opened new possibilities in the field of medicine. Scientists are now able to develop personalized treatments based on an individual's genetic makeup. These innovations promise to improve the effectiveness of medical interventions and reduce side effects, heralding a new era of precision medicine.

What is the main benefit of personalized treatments mentioned in the passage?

A) Lower healthcare costs
B) Improved effectiveness and reduced side effects
C) Faster recovery times
D) Universal access to healthcare

The correct answer is B - improved effectiveness and reduced side effects. The passage highlights how personalized treatments based on genetic makeup can enhance medical interventions.

QUESTION 3:

In her latest novel, the author explores themes of identity and belonging through the experiences of her protagonist, who is navigating life in a foreign country. The character's journey is marked by moments of self-discovery and cultural adaptation, ultimately leading to a deeper understanding of her own identity and place in the world.

What are the main themes explored in the author's novel according to the passage?

A) Adventure and excitement
B) Identity and belonging
C) Love and betrayal
D) Mystery and suspense

The correct answer is B - identity and belonging. The passage describes how the novel delves into the protagonist's experiences with identity and belonging.

QUESTION 4:

The practice of mindfulness has gained popularity in recent years as a way to reduce stress and improve overall well-being. Mindfulness involves focusing on the present moment and accepting one's thoughts and feelings without judgment. Research has shown that regular mindfulness practice can lead to better mental health and enhanced quality of life.

According to the passage, what is a key aspect of mindfulness practice?

A) Ignoring negative thoughts
B) Focusing on the present moment
C) Setting long-term goals
D) Analyzing past experiences

The correct answer is B - focusing on the present moment. The passage explains that mindfulness involves being present and accepting thoughts and feelings without judgment.

QUESTION 5:

The agricultural revolution brought about significant changes in human society. With the advent of farming, communities were able to settle in one place and develop complex social structures. This shift from a nomadic lifestyle to settled agriculture led to the growth of cities and the rise of civilizations.

What major change did the agricultural revolution bring about?

A) Increased nomadic lifestyle
B) Development of settled communities and cities
C) Decline in social structures
D) Decrease in population

The correct answer is B - development of settled communities and cities. The passage describes how the agricultural revolution allowed for the growth of permanent settlements and complex societies.

QUESTION 6:

Climate change poses a significant threat to global food security. Extreme weather events, such as droughts and floods, can devastate crops and disrupt food supply chains. Scientists and policymakers are working on strategies to make agriculture more resilient to these changes, ensuring that food production can meet the needs of a growing population.

What is the primary concern discussed in the passage regarding climate change?

A) Increased economic growth
B) Threat to global food security
C) Decrease in technology advancements

D) Improvement in agricultural yields

The correct answer is B - threat to global food security. The passage focuses on how climate change impacts agriculture and food supply chains.

QUESTION 7:

The discovery of antibiotics revolutionized medicine in the 20th century, providing effective treatments for bacterial infections. However, the overuse and misuse of antibiotics have led to the emergence of antibiotic-resistant bacteria. This growing problem requires urgent attention to develop new treatments and promote responsible antibiotic use.

What is the main issue related to antibiotics mentioned in the passage?

A) Lack of availability
B) Emergence of antibiotic-resistant bacteria
C) Decrease in bacterial infections
D) Overproduction of antibiotics

The correct answer is B - emergence of antibiotic-resistant bacteria. The passage discusses the consequences of overusing antibiotics and the need for new treatments.

QUESTION 8:

The rise of social media has transformed how people communicate and share information. While it has enabled greater connectivity and the rapid dissemination of news, it has also contributed to the spread of misinformation. Users must critically evaluate the information they encounter online to avoid being misled by false or biased content.

What is one negative impact of social media mentioned in the passage?

A) Decreased connectivity
B) Spread of misinformation
C) Reduced access to news
D) Limited sharing of information

The correct answer is B - spread of misinformation. The passage highlights how social media can contribute to the dissemination of false or biased information.

QUESTION 9:

The concept of sustainable tourism emphasizes the need to minimize the environmental and cultural impact of travel. Sustainable tourism practices include supporting local economies, reducing waste, and preserving natural and cultural heritage sites. Travelers are encouraged to make conscious choices that benefit both the environment and local communities.

What is a key principle of sustainable tourism according to the passage?

A) Maximizing tourist numbers

B) Supporting local economies and reducing waste
C) Expanding commercial tourism
D) Focusing solely on luxury experiences

The correct answer is B - supporting local economies and reducing waste. The passage describes sustainable tourism practices that benefit the environment and local communities.

QUESTION 10:

The field of renewable energy storage has seen significant advancements in recent years. Improved battery technologies allow for better storage of energy generated from renewable sources like solar and wind. These innovations are crucial for ensuring a stable and reliable energy supply, even when the sun isn't shining or the wind isn't blowing.

What advancement in renewable energy is highlighted in the passage?

A) Increased use of fossil fuels
B) Improved battery technologies for energy storage
C) Decrease in solar and wind energy production
D) Expansion of non-renewable energy sources

The correct answer is B - improved battery technologies for energy storage. The passage focuses on advancements in energy storage that enhance the reliability of renewable energy sources.

SUBMIT A REVIEW

Did these pages help, inspire, or bring you value in any way? If so, we'd love to hear your thoughts through an honest review on Amazon. Your feedback is incredibly valuable to us!

It's very simple and only takes a few minutes:

1. Go to the "My Orders" page on Amazon and search the book.
2. Select "Write a product review".
3. Select a Star Rating.
4. Optionally, add text, photos, or videos and select Submit.

CHAPTER 4
WRITING AND GRAMMAR SKILLS

Strong writing and language skills are essential for success on the SAT® and beyond. This chapter will provide an in-depth look at the key components of effective writing, including grammar and usage, sentence structure and punctuation, and contextual vocabulary and expression. We'll break down essential rules and guidelines, identify common pitfalls to avoid, and provide targeted strategies and practice exercises to help you refine your skills and excel on the Writing and Language section of the SAT®.

GRAMMAR AND USAGE

A solid foundation in English grammar and proper usage is critical for clear, correct writing. Let's review some of the most important grammar rules to know:

Subject-Verb Agreement

The subject and verb in a sentence must agree in number (singular or plural). A singular subject takes a singular verb, while a plural subject requires a plural verb.

Examples:

- She walks to school every day. (singular subject and verb)
- They walk to school every day. (plural subject and verb)

Common pitfalls:

- Sentences that start with "there" or "here": The subject follows the verb in these constructions.
  - There are three books on the shelf. ("books" is the plural subject)
- Collective nouns can be singular or plural depending on the context.
  - The team is practicing today. (singular - acting as one unit)
  - The team are putting on their uniforms. (plural - acting as separate individuals)
- Compound subjects joined by "and" are typically plural. Those joined by "or" or "nor" match the number of the subject closest to the verb.
  - Ava and Liam are coming to the party.
  - Either Ava or Liam is responsible for bringing dessert.

Pronoun-Antecedent

Agreement Pronouns must agree with their antecedents (the nouns they refer to) in number, gender, and person.

Examples:

- Each student should bring his or her notebook to class. (singular antecedent, matching singular pronouns)
- All applicants must submit their resumes by Friday. (plural antecedent, plural pronoun)

Common pitfalls:

- Indefinite pronouns (e.g. everybody, somebody, anyone) are singular and take singular verbs and pronouns.
  - Everyone should do his or her best.
- Collective nouns (e.g. team, family, group) can be singular or plural based on whether the group is acting as a unit or as individuals.

- The committee is meeting to vote on the proposal. It will announce its decision tomorrow.
- The committee are divided in their opinions. They will each submit an individual vote.

Verb Tense and Form

Verbs should maintain consistent tense within a sentence or passage and use the appropriate form.

Examples:

- She walked to the store and bought milk. (simple past tense)
- They have been studying for the exam all week. (present perfect progressive tense)
- If I were you, I would apologize for the mistake. (subjunctive mood)

Common pitfalls:

- Shifting verb tense unnecessarily within a sentence or paragraph.
  - Incorrect: She walks to the store and bought milk.
  - Correct: She walked to the store and bought milk.
- Misusing irregular verb forms.
  - Incorrect: He has went to the gym already.
  - Correct: He has gone to the gym already.
- Confusing the subjunctive mood (used for wishes, hypotheticals, or demands) with the past tense.
  - Incorrect: If I was rich, I would travel the world.
  - Correct: If I were rich, I would travel the world.

Parallel Structure

Phrases, clauses, or items in a series should maintain a consistent (parallel) grammatical form.

Examples:

- Incorrect: I enjoy hiking, swimming, and to fish.
- Correct: I enjoy hiking, swimming, and fishing. (three gerunds)
- Incorrect: The teacher asked us to read the chapter, taking notes, and we discussed the main ideas.
- Correct: The teacher asked us to read the chapter, take notes, and discuss the main ideas. (three parallel infinitive phrases)

Strategies for improvement:

1. Read extensively to expose yourself to proper grammar and usage in context. Pay attention to how authors structure their sentences.
2. Practice identifying and correcting common grammar errors in your own writing and sample passages.

3. Use grammar resources like textbooks, online guides, and practice exercises to reinforce your understanding of the rules.
4. When in doubt, simplify. Break complex sentences into shorter, clearer ones.
5. Proofread carefully, reading your work aloud to catch awkward phrasing or inconsistencies.

SENTENCE STRUCTURE AND PUNCTUATION

Effective sentence structure and punctuation are key to conveying your ideas clearly and coherently. Here are some guidelines and strategies to keep in mind:

Types of Sentences

Simple sentences contain one independent clause.

- I love reading mystery novels.

Compound sentences join two or more independent clauses with a coordinating conjunction (for, and, nor, but, or, yet, so) or a semicolon.

- I love reading mystery novels, and my sister prefers science fiction.
- I finished my homework; now I can relax.

Complex sentences have one independent clause and one or more dependent clauses.

- Although it was raining heavily, we enjoyed our hike in the mountains.

Compound-complex sentences contain two or more independent clauses and at least one dependent clause.

- I wanted to visit the museum, but my friend suggested going to the movies; we compromised by doing both since we had enough time.

Varying your sentence types creates a more engaging, dynamic writing style. Too many simple sentences can feel choppy, while too many long, complex sentences may be difficult to follow.

Punctuation

Commas

Use commas to separate items in a series, to set off nonessential clauses or phrases, and to join two independent clauses with a coordinating conjunction.

- I bought bread, milk, and eggs at the store.
- My brother, who lives in New York, is visiting next week.
- I wanted to go for a run, but it started raining.

Semicolons

Use semicolons to join closely related independent clauses or to separate items in a series that already contain commas.

- I have a big test tomorrow; I need to study tonight.
- The conference will be attended by representatives from Seattle, Washington; Portland, Oregon; and Vancouver, Canada.

Colons

Use colons to introduce a list, an explanation or example, or a quotation.

- Please bring the following items: sleeping bag, pillow, and toiletries.
- The reason was simple: we were out of time.
- Shakespeare wrote: "To be, or not to be, that is the question."

Dashes and parentheses

Use dashes or parentheses to set off nonessential information or abrupt interruptions.

- My sister—the one who lives in Chicago—is getting married this summer.
- I love reading (especially mystery novels) in my free time.

Apostrophes

Use apostrophes to show possession or to form contractions.

- Sarah's brother is joining us for dinner.
- That's the best movie I've seen in years!

Quotation marks

Use quotation marks to enclose direct quotations or titles of short works like poems, articles, or episodes.

- "I have a dream," said Martin Luther King Jr. in his famous speech.
- My favorite poem is "The Road Not Taken" by Robert Frost.

Strategies for improvement:

1. Read your writing aloud to identify run-on sentences, fragments, or awkward constructions. Revise for clarity and flow.
2. Use a mix of sentence types and lengths to create variety and keep your reader engaged.
3. Practice proper punctuation by writing sample sentences or correcting deliberately flawed passages.
4. Pay attention to how authors use punctuation effectively in published works.
5. When in doubt, consult a punctuation guide or handbook for specific rules and examples.

Coherence and Transitions

In addition to varied sentence structures, effective writing uses transitional words and phrases to link ideas and create coherence within and between paragraphs.

Types of transitions:

- Addition: and, also, furthermore, moreover, in addition
- Contrast: but, however, on the other hand, in contrast, nevertheless
- Cause and effect: because, since, consequently, as a result, therefore
- Sequence: first, second, next, then, finally
- Example: for example, for instance, specifically, to illustrate

Transitions help guide the reader through your argument or narrative, signaling the relationships between ideas and creating a logical flow.

Example

Revise the following passage for better coherence and flow by adding transitions and varied sentence structures:

I love playing soccer. It is a great way to stay fit. Soccer is a team sport. You have to work together with your teammates. Communication is key. You need to be able to strategize and execute plays. Soccer is also a lot of fun. I enjoy the competitive aspect of the game. I always feel a rush of adrenaline when I step onto the field.

Possible revision

I love playing soccer because it is not only a great way to stay fit but also an exciting team sport. On the field, you have to work closely with your teammates, communicating effectively to strategize and execute plays. Good communication is key to success in soccer. Moreover, the competitive aspect of the game is thrilling; I always feel a rush of adrenaline when I step onto the field, ready to give my all and contribute to my team's success. In short, soccer combines the benefits of physical fitness with the joy of collaboration and competition, making it a truly enjoyable pastime.

CONTEXTUAL VOCABULARY AND EFFECTIVE EXPRESSION

A robust, context-appropriate vocabulary allows you to express your ideas with precision and clarity. Here are some strategies for expanding your vocabulary and using language effectively:

Vocabulary in Context

Pay attention to how words are used in context, noting their connotations and the subtle differences between synonyms.

Example:

The words "slim," "thin," "slender," and "skinny" all describe someone who is not overweight, but each has a slightly different connotation:

- "Slim" and "slender" are generally positive, suggesting an attractive, healthy physique.
- "Thin" is more neutral, simply describing a person's physical appearance.
- "Skinny" can sometimes have a negative connotation, implying that someone is too thin or underweight.

Use context clues to infer the meaning of unfamiliar words.

- Definition context clues directly define the word in the sentence.
  - An "omnivore" is an animal that eats both plants and meat.
- Synonym context clues provide a word with a similar meaning.
  - The hikers were fatigued after their long trek; they were exhausted from the arduous journey.
    - Antonym context clues offer a word with the opposite meaning.
  - While some people are loquacious and talkative, others are more taciturn and reserved.
- Example context clues illustrate the meaning of the word through an example or explanation.
  - Iguanas, komodo dragons, and chameleons are all examples of reptiles.

Effective Expression

Use vivid, descriptive language to paint a clear picture in the reader's mind.

- Instead of: The sunset was beautiful.
- Try: The sky was set ablaze with streaks of vibrant orange and deep red as the sun dipped below the horizon.

Employ figurative language like similes, metaphors, and personification to add depth and interest to your writing.

- Simile: Her eyes sparkled like diamonds in the sunlight.
- Metaphor: The moon was a ghostly galleon tossed upon cloudy seas.
- Personification: The wind whispered secrets through the rustling leaves.

Choose strong, active verbs to convey action and create a sense of immediacy.

- Instead of: The dog was running quickly across the yard.
- Try: The dog sprinted across the yard.

Avoid clichés and overused phrases, opting for fresh, original language instead.

- Instead of: It was a dark and stormy night.
- Try: Lightning slashed through the ink-black sky as thunder rattled the windows.

Strategies for vocabulary development:

JUPITER DIGITAL EXAM PREP

1. Read extensively across various genres and subjects to encounter new words in context.
2. Keep a vocabulary journal to record new words, their definitions, and example sentences.
3. Use flashcards or online tools like Quizlet to practice and reinforce your vocabulary.
4. Play word games like Scrabble, Boggle, or crossword puzzles to engage with language in a fun, challenging way.
5. Incorporate newly learned words into your writing and conversation to solidify your understanding and retention.

PRACTICE EXERCISE

QUESTION 1:

Which revision would improve the clarity of the following sentence?

Original Sentence: "The conference was attended by many people who were interested in the latest developments in technology and had many discussions on the new innovations that were presented."

  A) "The conference attracted numerous technology enthusiasts and featured discussions on the latest innovations."
  B) "The conference was attended by many people who were interested in new innovations, and many discussions were had on the latest developments in technology."
  C) "Many people interested in technology attended the conference, where numerous discussions took place on the latest innovations."
  D) "The conference had many discussions on the new developments in technology, which were attended by many people."

Answer: A) "The conference attracted numerous technology enthusiasts and featured discussions on the latest innovations."

QUESTION 2:

Which sentence is the best choice for a formal research paper introduction?

  A) "A lot of people think climate change is a serious issue, and this paper will explain why it matters."
  B) "Climate change is a pressing issue that has significant implications for our environment, economy, and future generations. This paper will explore these impacts in detail."
  C) "The topic of climate change is pretty important, so let's see what we can find out about it in this paper."
  D) "Climate change has been talked about a lot recently. In this paper, we'll look at why it's important."

Answer: B) "Climate change is a pressing issue that has significant implications for our environment, economy, and future generations. This paper will explore these impacts in detail."

QUESTION 3:

Which of the following sentences is an effective thesis statement for an essay on renewable energy?

- A) "Renewable energy sources are good for the environment."
- B) "There are various types of renewable energy, including solar, wind, and hydro power."
- C) "Investing in renewable energy is crucial for reducing our dependence on fossil fuels and combating climate change."
- D) "Renewable energy can be expensive, but it has many benefits."

Answer: C) "Investing in renewable energy is crucial for reducing our dependence on fossil fuels and combating climate change."

QUESTION 4:

How can the following sentence be revised to avoid redundancy?

Original Sentence: "The new policy is expected to bring about significant improvements in employee productivity and will lead to greater efficiency in the workplace."

- A) "The new policy is expected to enhance both employee productivity and workplace efficiency."
- B) "The new policy is expected to bring about significant improvements and will also lead to greater efficiency in the workplace."
- C) "The new policy is expected to significantly improve employee productivity and workplace efficiency."
- D) "The new policy will bring about improvements in productivity and greater efficiency in the workplace."

Answer: C) "The new policy is expected to significantly improve employee productivity and workplace efficiency."

QUESTION 5:

Which revision would enhance the engagement of the following sentence?

Original Sentence: "The marketing campaign was designed to increase sales and attract more customers to the store."

- A) "The marketing campaign aimed to boost sales and draw more customers into the store."
- B) "The marketing campaign was focused on sales increase and customer attraction."
- C) "The campaign's design was centered around increasing store sales and customer attraction."

D) "The store's marketing campaign was intended for sales improvement and customer increase."

Answer: A) "The marketing campaign aimed to boost sales and draw more customers into the store."

SUBMIT A REVIEW

Did these pages help, inspire, or bring you value in any way? If so, we'd love to hear your thoughts through an honest review on Amazon. Your feedback is incredibly valuable to us!

It's very simple and only takes a few minutes:

1. Go to the "My Orders" page on Amazon and search the book.
2. Select "Write a product review".
3. Select a Star Rating.
4. Optionally, add text, photos, or videos and select Submit.

PART III
MATH

CHAPTER 5
HEART OF ALGEBRA

Algebra is a fundamental branch of mathematics that deals with the manipulation of variables and equations. In the SAT® Math section, the Heart of Algebra subscore assesses your understanding of linear equations, inequalities, and systems. Mastering these concepts is crucial for success on the SAT® and in various real-world applications. In this chapter, we will break down the essential algebraic concepts, provide step-by-step problem-solving strategies, highlight common mistakes to avoid, and offer a series of practice questions designed to build your algebraic skills.

LINEAR EQUATIONS AND SYSTEMS

Linear Equations

A linear equation is an equation that can be written in the form ax + b = c, where a, b, and c are constants (real numbers), and x is a variable. The graph of a linear equation is a straight line.

Example:

2x + 3 = 7 is a linear equation.

To solve a linear equation, isolate the variable on one side of the equation by performing the same operation on both sides.

Example:

Solve for x: 2x + 3 = 7

2x = 7 - 3

2x = 4

x = 4 ÷ 2

x = 2

Therefore, the solution to the equation 2x + 3 = 7 is x = 2.

Linear Inequalities

A linear inequality is similar to a linear equation but uses inequality symbols (<, ≤, >, ≥) instead of an equals sign. The graph of a linear inequality is a region on one side of a straight line.

Example:

3x - 1 > 5 is a linear inequality.

To solve a linear inequality, follow the same steps as solving a linear equation. However, if you multiply or divide both sides by a negative number, you must reverse the inequality symbol.

Example:

Solve for x: 3x - 1 > 5

3x > 5 + 1

3x > 6

x > 6 ÷ 3

x > 2

Therefore, the solution to the inequality 3x - 1 > 5 is x > 2.

Systems of Linear Equations

A system of linear equations is a set of two or more linear equations with the same variables. The solution to a system of linear equations is the point (or points) where the graphs of the equations intersect.

There are three main methods for solving systems of linear equations:

1. Graphing
2. Substitution
3. Elimination

Graphing Method

To solve a system of linear equations by graphing, follow these steps:

a. Graph each equation on the same coordinate plane.
b. Identify the point(s) of intersection, if any.
c. The coordinates of the point(s) of intersection are the solution to the system.

Example

Solve the system of linear equations by graphing:

$y = 2x - 1$

$y = -x + 3$

Graph the equations and find the point of intersection:

The lines intersect at (2, 3).

Therefore, the solution to the system is x = 2 and y = 3.

Substitution Method

To solve a system of linear equations using substitution, follow these steps:

a. Choose one equation and solve for one variable in terms of the other.
b. Substitute the expression from step (a) into the other equation.
c. Solve the resulting equation for the remaining variable.
d. Substitute the value from step (c) into the expression from step (a) to find the value of the other variable.
e. Check your solution by substituting the values into both original equations.

Example

Solve the system of linear equations using substitution:

$2x + y = 7$

$x - y = 1$

Step a: Solve the second equation for x.

$x - y = 1$

$x = y + 1$

Step b: Substitute $x = y + 1$ into the first equation.

$2(y + 1) + y = 7$

$2y + 2 + y = 7$

$3y + 2 = 7$

Step c: Solve the resulting equation for y.

$3y + 2 = 7$

$3y = 7 - 2$

$3y = 5$

$y = 5 \div 3$

Step d: Substitute $y = 5/3$ into $x = y + 1$.

$x = (5/3) + 1$

$x = 5/3 + 3/3$

$x = 8/3$

Therefore, the solution to the system is $x = 8/3$ and $y = 5/3$.

Elimination Method

To solve a system of linear equations using elimination, follow these steps:

   a. Multiply one or both equations by a constant to make the coefficients of one variable equal in magnitude but opposite in sign.
   b. Add the equations from step (a) to eliminate one variable.
   c. Solve the resulting equation for the remaining variable.
   d. Substitute the value from step (c) into one of the original equations to find the value of the other variable.
   e. Check your solution by substituting the values into both original equations.

Example:

Solve the system of linear equations using elimination:

$2x + 3y = 11$

$x - 3y = -5$

Step a: The coefficients of y are already equal in magnitude but opposite in sign, so no multiplication is needed.

Step b: Add the equations to eliminate y.

$(2x + 3y) + (x - 3y) = 11 + (-5)$

$(2x + x) + (3y - 3y) = 11 - 5$

$3x + 0 = 6$

$3x = 6$

Step c: Solve the resulting equation for x.

$3x = 6$

$x = 6 \div 3$

$x = 2$

Step d: Substitute x = 2 into one of the original equations to find y.

$2(2) + 3y = 11$

$4 + 3y = 11$

$3y = 11 - 4$

$3y = 7$

$y = 7 \div 3$

Therefore, the solution to the system is x = 2 and y = 7/3.

PROBLEM-SOLVING TECHNIQUES

When tackling algebraic problems, it is essential to follow a structured approach to ensure accuracy and efficiency. The first step is to read and understand the problem thoroughly. Identify the given information and the unknown values, and determine the relationships between them. If applicable, visualize the problem by sketching a diagram or picture to help you better grasp the situation.

Once you have a clear understanding of the problem, develop a plan by breaking it down into smaller, more manageable steps. Choose an appropriate strategy or method based on the problem type and given information. Strategies may include solving linear equations or inequalities, solving systems of linear equations using graphing, substitution, or elimination, creating equations or expressions based on the problem context, or using formulas and properties specific to the problem situation.

With a plan in place, proceed to solve the problem by executing the steps you have outlined. Show your work and keep your steps organized to avoid confusion and errors. Simplify expressions and solve equations or inequalities as needed, and double-check your calculations to prevent arithmetic mistakes.

After arriving at a solution, review and check your work to ensure that it answers the original question. Substitute your solution back into the original equation, inequality, or system to verify its correctness. Consider whether your solution makes sense in the context of the problem. If time permits, try solving the problem using an alternative method to confirm your answer.

Common Mistakes to Avoid

While solving algebraic problems, it is crucial to be aware of common mistakes and take steps to avoid them. One of the most frequent errors is misreading or misinterpreting the problem statement. To prevent this, take the time to carefully read and understand the problem before attempting to solve it, paying close attention to key phrases, units, and relationships between the given information.

Another common mistake is incorrectly translating word problems into equations or expressions. Practice identifying key words and phrases that indicate mathematical operations, such as "sum," "difference," "product," "quotient," "more than," or "less than." When setting up equations, assign variables to unknown quantities and clearly define what each variable represents.

Mixing up the order of operations (PEMDAS) is another error that can lead to incorrect solutions. Remember the correct order: Parentheses, Exponents, Multiplication and Division (left to right), Addition and Subtraction (left to right). Use parentheses to group expressions and clarify the intended order of operations.

Arithmetic errors can also derail your problem-solving efforts. Take your time and double-check your calculations, and use estimation to quickly check the reasonableness of your answer.

When working with equations and inequalities, be sure to distribute negative signs or coefficients correctly. When multiplying or dividing both sides of an equation or inequality by a negative number, apply the negative sign to all terms and remember to reverse the inequality symbol when necessary.

Mishandling fractional coefficients or constants is another pitfall to avoid. Be careful when performing operations with fractions, especially when multiplying or dividing both sides of an equation or inequality by a fraction. Simplify fractions and convert between improper fractions and mixed numbers as needed.

Finally, be mindful of the properties of equality and inequality. When solving equations, remember that performing the same operation on both sides maintains equality. However, when solving inequalities, multiplying or dividing both sides by a negative number reverses the inequality symbol.

PRACTICE EXERCISES

Exercise 1

1. Which of the following is an example of a linear equation?

    a) $x2 + 3x = 5$
    b) $3x - 5 = 0$
    c) $y = x3$
    d) $2x + 4 = 1$

The correct answer is b) 3x - 5 = 0. This is a linear equation because it contains variables raised to the first power only.

2. What is the solution method used to solve the linear equation 4x - 2 = 10?

    a) Addition
    b) Substitution
    c) Multiplication
    d) Division

The correct answer is d) Division. To solve the equation, we add 2 to both sides to get 4x = 12, then divide both sides by 4 to isolate x.

3. What is the graph of a linear equation?

    a) A circle
    b) A parabola
    c) A straight line
    d) An exponential curve

The correct answer is c) A straight line. Linear equations have a constant rate of change, so they graph as straight lines when plotted.

4. How many solutions can a system of linear equations have?

    a) 0 or 1
    b) 1 or 2
    c) 0, 1 or infinitely many
    d) Only 1

The correct answer is c) 0, 1 or infinitely many. Systems of linear equations can have no solution (parallel lines), a unique solution (intersecting lines) or infinitely many solutions (coincident lines).

5. What technique adds or subtracts equations when solving a system of linear equations?

a) Substitution
b) Elimination
c) Division
d) Multiplication

The correct answer is b) Elimination. Adding or subtracting equations allows like terms to be cancelled out or eliminated, helping to solve for variables.

6. What does the acronym "LIES" stand for in solving systems of linear equations?

a) Line Intersect to Extract Solution
b) Linear Intersections Equal Solutions
c) Lines Intersect is Equation Solution
d) Linear Inequality Eliminate Substitution

The correct answer is b) Linear Intersections Equal Solutions. This mnemonic represents the concepts used to solve systems of linear equations graphically or algebraically.

7. What type of system has lines that intersect at a single point?

a) Dependent
b) Independent
c) Consistent
d) Inconsistent

The correct answer is c) Consistent. A consistent system has lines that intersect at one point, meaning there is a single solution.

8. What property of linear equations allows them to be graphed as straight lines?

a) Single variable term
b) Constant rate of change
c) No variable exponents
d) Both a and c

The correct answer is d) Both a and c. Linear equations are graphed as lines because they contain variables raised to the first power only, with a constant rate of change.

9. What term describes a linear equation containing only one variable?

a) Polynomial
b) Monomial
c) Univariate
d) Binomial

The correct answer is c) Univariate. An equation containing only one variable is called univariate, since it deals with a single variable.

10. What technique can be used to solve a 2x2 system that produces a unique solution?

    a) Graphing
    b) Addition
    c) Elimination
    d) Multiplication

The correct answer is c) Elimination. The elimination method can algebraically solve a 2x2 system by adding or subtracting rows to remove one of the variables.

Exercise 2

1. What is the solution to the equation 5x - 3 = 12?

    a) $x = 3$
    b) $x = 4$
    c) $x = -1$
    d) $x = 0.5$

The answer is a) x = 3. To solve we add 3 to both sides to get $5x = 15$. Then divide both sides by 5.

2. Find the value of x given: 2x + 3 = 5

    a) 1
    b) 2
    c) -1
    d) 0

The answer is a) 1. To solve we subtract 3 from both sides to get $2x = 2$. Then divide both sides by 2.

3. Solve for x: 3x - 2 = 7

    a) $x = 3$
    b) $x = 2$
    c) $x = 5$
    d) $x = 1$

The answer is a) x = 3. To solve we add 2 to both sides to get 3x = 9. Then divide both sides by 3.

4. What is the y-intercept of the line y = -2x + 5?

    a) -2
    b) 2
    c) 5
    d) -5

The answer is c) 5. The y-intercept is the value of y when $x = 0$. Substituting 0 for x gives $y = -2(0) + 5 = 5$.

5. Solve the system:

2x - y = 4

x + y = 5

    a) x = 2, y = 3
    b) x = 3, y = 2
    c) x = 1, y = 4
    d) x = -1, y = 6

The answer is a) x = 2, y = 3. Using elimination, we add the equations to eliminate y.

6. Solve for x: -3x + 6 = 12

    a) x = 3
    b) x = -4
    c) x = 2
    d) x = -2

The answer is d) -2. To solve we subtract 6 to both sides to get -3x = 6. Then divide both sides by -3.

7. Find the slope of the line with equation y = 3x + 1

    a) 1
    b) 3
    c) -3
    d) -1

The answer is b) 3. The slope is the coefficient of x.

8. Solve the system:

x - 2y = 4

3x + y = 5

    a) x = 2, y = -1
    b) x = 1, y = 2
    c) x = -1, y = 3
    d) x = 3, y = -2

The answer is a) x = 2, y = -1. Using elimination, we multiply the second equation by 3 and add to eliminate x.

9. Solve for x: 2x - 3 = 9

    a) x = 4
    b) x = 6
    c) x = 3
    d) x = 5

The answer is b) x = 6. To solve we add 3 from both sides to get 2x = 12. Then divide both sides by 2.

10. Solve the system:

4x - 2y = 12

x + 2y = 8

  a) x = 3, y = 2
  b) x = 4, y = 2
  c) x = 1, y = 1
  d) x = 4, y = -1

The answer is b) x = 4, y = 2. Adding the equations eliminates y, then we substitute back to find y.

⭐ ⭐ ⭐ ⭐ ⭐

SUBMIT A REVIEW

Did these pages help, inspire, or bring you value in any way? If so, we'd love to hear your thoughts through an honest review on Amazon. Your feedback is incredibly valuable to us!

It's very simple and only takes a few minutes:

1. Go to the "My Orders" page on Amazon and search the book.
2. Select "Write a product review".
3. Select a Star Rating.
4. Optionally, add text, photos, or videos and select Submit.

CHAPTER 6
PROBLEM SOLVING AND DATA ANALYSIS

Chapter 6 is about learning important skills to understand and use numbers to solve real-world problems. Students will learn how to look closely at different types of data visuals like graphs and charts, and identify patterns or unusual points that help make decisions.

A big part of this chapter is understanding graphs and charts. Students will go beyond just reading the numbers to understanding the story those numbers tell. They will learn to see what different graphs and charts are really saying, while also being careful not to be misled by their own biases.

The chapter also focuses on key ideas like ratios, percentages, and proportions, which are important in math, science, and everyday life. Students will learn to solve word problems involving rates, discounts, mixtures, and changes in scale.

Real-life examples will help students practice their new skills. They will look at things like population surveys, financial reports, and experimental results to see how data is used in real-world situations. Practice exercises will help students evaluate everyday scenarios and improve their ability to find useful information.

By the end of the chapter, students will be better at understanding quantitative information from sources like media infographics or surveys. These skills will help them in future statistical courses and make them better at thinking critically about numbers they see in everyday life.

INTERPRETING GRAPHS AND CHARTS

Graphs and charts are powerful tools for visualizing and communicating data. Common types of graphs and charts you may encounter on the SAT® include:

Line Graphs

Line graphs are used to display trends or changes in data over time.

Example

A line graph showing the population growth of a city over a decade.

How it looks:

- X-Axis: Represents time (years).
- Y-Axis: Represents population size.
- Line: Connects data points that show the population at different years.

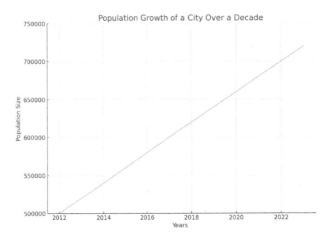

Bar Graphs

Bar graphs are used to compare data across different categories or groups.

Example:

A bar graph comparing the average test scores of students in different grade levels.

How it looks:

- X-Axis: Represents grade levels (e.g., Grade 1, Grade 2, Grade 3).
- Y-Axis: Represents average test scores.
- Bars: Each bar's height shows the average score for that grade level.

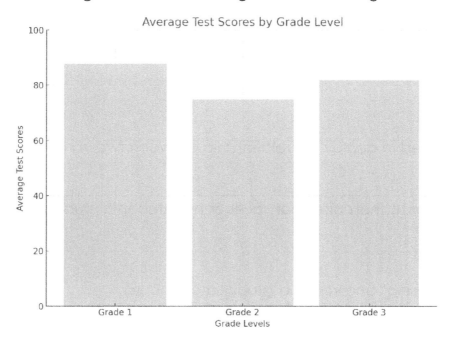

Pie Charts

Pie charts are used to show the proportional composition of a whole.

Example:

A pie chart illustrating the distribution of a company's expenses by category.

How it looks:

- Circle: Represents the whole company's expenses.
- Slices: Each slice shows the proportion of total expenses spent on different categories (e.g., salaries, rent, supplies).

Company's Expenses Distribution

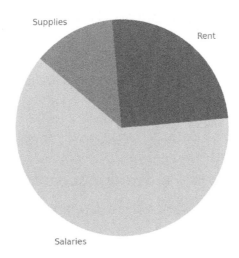

Scatterplots

Scatterplots are used to display the relationship between two variables.

Example:

A scatterplot showing the correlation between a student's study time and their exam scores.

How it looks:

- X-Axis: Represents one variable (study time in hours).
- Y-Axis: Represents another variable (exam scores).
- Dots: Each dot represents one student's study time and their exam score.

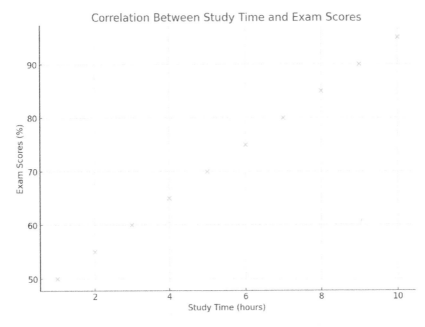

In this example, you see that as study time increases, exam scores tend to increase too, showing a positive relationship between study time and exam scores.

When interpreting graphs and charts, consider the following:

- Read the title, labels, and legend to understand the context and what the data represents
- Identify the dependent and independent variables (if applicable)
- Observe patterns, trends, and outliers in the data
- Draw conclusions based on the information presented

Example:

A line graph shows the average monthly temperature in a city over a year. The x-axis represents the months, and the y-axis represents the temperature in degrees Fahrenheit. The line starts at 32°F in January, rises to a peak of 85°F in July, and then decreases to 35°F in December.

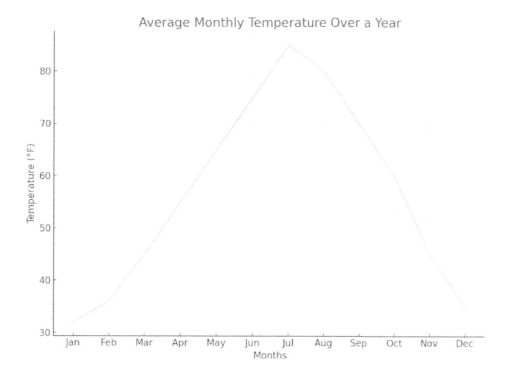

Questions:

1. In which month is the average temperature the highest? Answer: July
2. What is the approximate difference between the average temperature in January and the average temperature in July? Answer: 85°F - 32°F = 53°F

WORKING WITH RATIOS, PERCENTAGES, AND PROPORTIONAL RELATIONSHIPS

Ratios, percentages, and proportional relationships are essential concepts in problem-solving and data analysis. They are frequently tested on the SAT® and have numerous real-world applications. In this section, we'll explore these concepts in detail, provide practical information, and illustrate their use with examples.

Ratios

A ratio is a comparison of two quantities, typically expressed as a fraction, with a colon, or using the word "to." Ratios can compare parts to parts, parts to a whole, or one whole to another whole.

Examples:

- In a class of 30 students, the ratio of boys to girls is 2:3 (read as "two to three").
- The ratio of red marbles to blue marbles in a bag is 1/4 (read as "one to four" or "one-fourth").
- The scale on a map is 1:50,000, meaning one unit on the map represents 50,000 units in reality.

When working with ratios, it's essential to ensure that the quantities being compared have the same units. If the units differ, you must convert them before setting up the ratio.

Example

A recipe calls for 3 cups of flour and 2 pints of milk. Express the ratio of flour to milk in the recipe.

- Step 1: Convert pints to cups. 1 pint = 2 cups, so 2 pints = 4 cups.
- Step 2: Express the ratio of flour to milk as 3:4 or 3/4.

Ratios can be scaled up or down by multiplying or dividing both quantities by the same number. This is useful when solving problems involving proportional relationships.

Example

A recipe that serves 4 people calls for 2 cups of rice and 3 cups of water. If you want to make enough for 6 people, how much rice and water should you use?

- Step 1: Determine the scale factor. To serve 6 people instead of 4, you need to multiply the quantities by 6/4 or 3/2.
- Step 2: Multiply the quantities by the scale factor.

  Rice: 2 cups × 3/2 = 3 cups

Water: 3 cups × 3/2 = 4.5 cups (or 4 1/2 cups)

Percentages

A percentage is a ratio expressed as a fraction of 100. It is denoted using the % symbol. Percentages are used to represent parts of a whole, where the whole is always 100%.

To convert a percentage to a decimal, divide it by 100. To convert a decimal to a percentage, multiply it by 100.

Examples:

- 25% = 25/100 = 0.25
- 0.8 = 0.8 × 100 = 80%

Percentages are often used to calculate parts of a whole, such as finding the amount of a discount, tax, or tip.

Example

A store offers a 30% discount on a $50 item. How much will you save, and what will be the final price?

- Step 1: Convert the percentage to a decimal. 30% = 0.30
- Step 2: Calculate the discount amount. $50 × 0.30 = $15
- Step 3: Calculate the final price. $50 - $15 = $35 You will save $15, and the final price will be $35.

Percentages can also be used to calculate percent change, which measures the relative change in a quantity over time.

Example

The price of a stock increased from $100 to $120. What is the percent increase?

- Step 1: Calculate the change in price. $120 - $100 = $20
- Step 2: Divide the change by the original price. $20 / $100 = 0.20
- Step 3: Convert the decimal to a percentage. 0.20 × 100 = 20% The percent increase in the stock price is 20%.

Proportional Relationships

Proportional relationships occur when two quantities are related by a constant ratio. In other words, as one quantity changes, the other quantity changes proportionally.

The constant ratio in a proportional relationship is called the constant of proportionality. It can be found by dividing one quantity by the other.

Example

A car travels 120 miles in 3 hours. Assuming the car maintains a constant speed, how far will it travel in 5 hours?

- Step 1: Determine the constant of proportionality (the car's speed). 120 miles / 3 hours = 40 miles per hour
- Step 2: Set up a proportion using the constant of proportionality. 40 miles/hour = x miles/5 hours, where x is the distance traveled in 5 hours.
- Step 3: Solve for x using cross multiplication. $40 \times 5 = 1 \times x$ 200 = x The car will travel 200 miles in 5 hours.

Proportional relationships can also be represented using equations in the form $y = kx$, where k is the constant of proportionality.

Example

The cost of printing posters is proportional to the number of posters printed. If 10 posters cost $30, write an equation representing the relationship between the cost (C) and the number of posters (n).

- Step 1: Determine the constant of proportionality (cost per poster). $30 / 10 posters = $3 per poster
- Step 2: Write the equation using the constant of proportionality. C = 3n, where C is the cost in dollars, and n is the number of posters.

PRACTICE EXERCISES

Exercise 1

1. When comparing two data sets, which measure of center would you use?

a) Mean
b) Median
c) Mode
d) Range

The answer is b) Median. When comparing two datasets, the median is the best measure of center as it is not influenced by outliers like the mean.

2. What type of graph is best for showing changes over time?

a) Pie chart
b) Bar graph
c) Line graph
d) Scatter plot

The answer is c) Line graph. A line graph best shows changes over time as it connects data points across a continuous timeline.

3. What does the y-axis typically represent on a line graph?

a) Categories
b) Time periods
c) Measurement values
d) Percentages

The answer is c) Measurement values. Typically the y-axis on a line graph represents the measurement values or quantities being tracked over time on the x-axis.

4. What type of graph is best for comparing parts to a whole?

a) Bar graph
b) Line graph
c) Pie chart
d) Scatter plot

The answer is c) Pie chart. A pie chart is best for comparing parts (slices) to the whole (full pie), showing what percentage each part is of the total.

5. What measure of variability calculates how far values are from the mean?

a) Range
b) Median
c) Interquartile range
d) Standard deviation

The answer is d) Standard deviation. Standard deviation calculates how far values typically are from the mean, providing a measure of variability or dispersion in the data.

6. When is it inappropriate to claim a causal relationship based on a graph?

a) With a pie chart
b) With a scatter plot
c) With a bar graph
d) With a line graph

The answer is b) With a scatter plot. A scatter plot only implies correlation, not causation, between two variables since a third variable could be influencing them.

7. What aspect of a graph should you check for accuracy?

a) Font size
b) Legend
c) Scale calibration
d) Title

The answer is c) Scale calibration. You should check the scale is accurately calibrated on the axes without exaggerating differences to avoid distortion.

8. What type of correlation does a diagonal line indicate on a scatter plot?

    a) Positive
    b) Negative
    c) None
    d) Either positive or negative

The answer is a) Positive. A diagonal line from bottom left to top right on a scatter plot indicates positive correlation between increasing variables.

9. What measures the middle value when data is sorted?

    a) Mean
    b) Median
    c) Mode
    d) Range

The answer is b) Median. The median is the middle value when a dataset is sorted numerically or alphabetically from lowest to highest.

10. When should alternative graph types be considered instead of a pie chart?

    a) To compare subsets
    b) To show values literally
    c) To depict one data point
    d) Only with 3-D graphs

The answer is a) To compare subsets. Alternative graphs like bar or stacked column charts are better than pie charts when you need to compare proportions within categorical subgroups rather than just the overall total.

Exercise 2:

1. If the ratio of boys to girls in a class is 3:5, what is the ratio in simplest form?

    a) 3:5
    b) 6:10
    c) 3/5
    d) 15:25

The correct answer is c) 3/5 - To put the ratio in simplest form, divide both the numerator and denominator by their greatest common factor which is 3.

2. What percentage of 80 is 32?

    a) 40%
    b) 32%
    c) 50%
    d) 20%

Correct option is a) 40% - To calculate a percentage, take the part (32) and divide by the whole (80) which is 0.4 or 40%.

3. If a recipe makes 8 servings and the ingredients are doubled, how many servings will it make?

    a) 8
    b) 12
    c) 16
    d) 4

Correct answer is c) 16 - When ingredients are doubled, recipes make twice as many servings. So doubling 8 makes 8 * 2 = 16 servings.

4. A $400 purchase was marked up by 25%. What was the original cost?

    a) $300
    b) $320
    c) $400
    d) $500

B is the right answer $325 - To calculate the original cost, take the sale price ($400) and divide by 1 + the markup percentage (1 + 0.25 = 1.25). So $400 / 1.25 = $320.

5. If 5 liters of concentrated juice makes 15 liters of drink, how many liters of drink can be made from 2 liters of concentrate?

    a) 5
    b) 6
    c) 30
    d) 10

D is the right answer 10 - Set up the ratio as a proportion: 5 liters concentrate / 15 liters drink = 2 liters concentrate / x liters drink. Cross multiply and solve for x.

6. Sprint spent 60% of its $100 million marketing budget on TV ads. How much did it spend on TV ads?

    a) $40 million
    b) $60 million
    c) $70 million
    d) $100 million

B is the right answer $60 million - 60% of $100 million is 0.6 * $100 million = $60 million

7. A recipe for cookies requires 2 cups of sugar. If the batch is tripled, how much sugar is needed?

    a) 2 cups
    b) 6 cups
    c) 4 cups
    d) 3 cups

B is the right answer 6 cups - Tripling the recipe triples all ingredients. The original recipe requires 2 cups so tripling is 2 * 3 = 6 cups.

8. 18 is what percentage of 60?

    a) 30%
    b) 15%
    c) 25%
    d) 20%

a is the right answer 30% - To calculate a percentage, take the part (18) and divide by the whole (60) which is 0.3 or 30%.

9. A company sold 125 widgets at $5 each. Using a 20% markup, what was the original cost of each widget?

    a) $5
    b) $4
    c) $4.25
    d) $4.16

d is the correct answer $4.16 - Original cost is sale price / (1 + markup%). So $5 / (1 + 0.2) = $5 / 1.2 = $4.16

10. Tasha drove 250 miles at an average speed of 50 mph. How many hours did she drive?

    a) 2.5 hours
    b) 5 hours
    c) 4 hours
    d) 2 hours

B is the right answer 5 hours – Use time formulae: Time= distance/speed = 250 miles / 50 mph.

SUBMIT A REVIEW

Did these pages help, inspire, or bring you value in any way? If so, we'd love to hear your thoughts through an honest review on Amazon. Your feedback is incredibly valuable to us!

It's very simple and only takes a few minutes:

1. Go to the "My Orders" page on Amazon and search the book.
2. Select "Write a product review".
3. Select a Star Rating.
4. Optionally, add text, photos, or videos and select Submit.

CHAPTER 7
PASSPORT TO ADVANCED MATH

This chapter explores quadratic algebra, going beyond the simpler linear relationships we studied earlier. Students will learn about quadratic expressions and functions, including how to identify their different forms: standard, factored, and vertex. A key part of this chapter is learning to graph quadratic functions by finding the axis of symmetry and x-intercepts.

To solve quadratic equations, students will use methods like factoring, taking square roots, and using the quadratic formula. They will also learn about the discriminant, which helps determine how many solutions a quadratic equation has and what type they are. Understanding these quadratic skills is important for many STEM applications that use quadratic or more complex expressions.

The chapter also introduces polynomial algebra, focusing on expressions with terms higher than the first degree, like binomials, trinomials, and other polynomial expressions. Students will learn to expand, factor, simplify, and perform basic operations on these expressions. By connecting polynomial functions to real-world situations that follow quadratic or higher-order patterns, students will build a deeper understanding.

Exercises in the chapter provide practice and application opportunities. By studying these advanced algebraic concepts, students will be well-prepared for further mathematical studies.

QUADRATIC EQUATIONS AND FUNCTIONS

A quadratic equation is an equation that can be written in the standard form $ax^2 + bx + c = 0$, where a, b, and c are real numbers, and $a \neq 0$. The solutions to a quadratic equation are called the roots or zeros of the equation.

There are several methods to solve quadratic equations:

Factoring

To solve a quadratic equation by factoring, follow these steps:

1. Write the equation in standard form: $ax^2 + bx + c = 0$
2. Factor the left side of the equation
3. Set each factor equal to zero and solve for x

Example

Solve $x^2 - 5x + 6 = 0$ by factoring.

Step 1: The equation is already in standard form.

Step 2: Factor the left side: $(x - 2)(x - 3) = 0$

Step 3: Set each factor equal to zero and solve:

$x - 2 = 0$ or $x - 3 = 0$

$x = 2$ or $x = 3$

The solutions are $x = 2$ and $x = 3$.

Quadratic Formula

The quadratic formula is a universal method to solve any quadratic equation. For an equation $ax^2 + bx + c = 0$, the quadratic formula is:

$$x = [-b \pm \sqrt{(b^2 - 4ac)}] / 2a$$

Example

Solve $2x^2 + 5x - 3 = 0$ using the quadratic formula.

Step 1: Identify the values of a, b, and c:

$a = 2, b = 5, c = -3$

Step 2: Substitute the values into the quadratic formula:

$x = [-5 \pm \sqrt{(5^2 - 4(2)(-3))}] / 2(2)$

$= [-5 \pm \sqrt{(25 + 24)}] / 4$

$= [-5 \pm \sqrt{49}] / 4$

$= (-5 \pm 7) / 4$

Step 3: Simplify:

$x = (-5 + 7) / 4$ or $(-5 - 7) / 4$

$= 2/4$ or $-12/4$

$= 1/2$ or -3

The solutions are $x = 1/2$ and $x = -3$.

Completing the Square

Completing the square is a method to solve quadratic equations and to convert a quadratic function into vertex form.

Example:

Solve $x^2 + 6x + 5 = 0$ by completing the square.

Step 1: Move the constant term to the right side:

$x^2 + 6x = -5$

Step 2: Divide the coefficient of x by 2 and square the result:

$(6/2)^2 = 3^2 = 9$

Step 3: Add the squared result to both sides of the equation:

x^2 + 6x + 9 = -5 + 9

x^2 + 6x + 9 = 4

Step 4: Factor the left side as a perfect square trinomial:

(x + 3)^2 = 4

Step 5: Take the square root of both sides:

x + 3 = ±2

Step 6: Solve for x:

x = -3 ± 2

x = -1 or x = -5

The solutions are x = -1 and x = -5.

Quadratic Functions

A quadratic function is a function of the form f(x) = ax^2 + bx + c, where a, b, and c are real numbers, and a ≠ 0. The graph of a quadratic function is a parabola.

Key features of a quadratic function:

- Axis of symmetry: The vertical line that passes through the vertex of the parabola. Its equation is x = -b / (2a).
- Vertex: The point where the parabola changes direction. It is either the minimum or maximum point of the function.
- y-intercept: The point where the parabola intersects the y-axis. It is found by evaluating f(0).
- x-intercepts (or roots): The points where the parabola intersects the x-axis. They are the solutions to the equation f(x) = 0.

Example:

Given the quadratic function f(x) = -2x^2 + 8x - 3, find the following:

a) Axis of symmetry
b) Vertex
c) y-intercept
d) x-intercepts

Solution:

a) Axis of symmetry: x = -b / (2a) = -8 / (2(-2)) = 2

The axis of symmetry is the line x = 2.

b) Vertex: To find the vertex, first find the x-coordinate using the axis of symmetry, then evaluate f(x) at that x-coordinate.

x-coordinate of vertex: x = 2

y-coordinate of vertex: $f(2) = -2(2)^2 + 8(2) - 3 = -8 + 16 - 3 = 5$

The vertex is (2, 5).

c) y-intercept: Evaluate f(0).

$f(0) = -2(0)^2 + 8(0) - 3 = -3$

The y-intercept is (0, -3).

d) x-intercepts: Solve the equation f(x) = 0.

$-2x^2 + 8x - 3 = 0$

Using the quadratic formula with a = -2, b = 8, and c = -3:

$x = [-8 \pm \sqrt{(8^2 - 4(-2)(-3))}] / 2(-2)$

$= [-8 \pm \sqrt{(64 + 24)}] / -4$

$= [-8 \pm \sqrt{88}] / -4$

$x_1 = (-8 + \sqrt{88}) / -4 \approx 0.3$

$x_2 = (-8 - \sqrt{88}) / -4 \approx 3.7$

The x-intercepts are approximately (0.3, 0) and (3.7, 0).

POLYNOMIAL ALGEBRA

A polynomial is an expression consisting of variables and coefficients combined using only the operations of addition, subtraction, multiplication, and non-negative integer exponents. The standard form of a polynomial is written in descending order of exponents, with terms grouped by exponent:

$a_n x^n + a_{(n-1)} x^{(n-1)} + ... + a_2 x^2 + a_1 x + a_0$

where $a_n, a_{(n-1)}, ..., a_2, a_1$, and a_0 are real numbers, and n is a non-negative integer.

Key terms:

- Degree: The highest exponent of the variable in the polynomial.
- Leading coefficient: The coefficient of the term with the highest exponent.
- Constant term: The term without a variable (a_0 in the standard form).

Operations with Polynomials

Addition and Subtraction

To add or subtract polynomials, combine like terms (terms with the same variables and exponents).

Example:

Add $(3x^2 - 2x + 1)$ and $(2x^2 + 5x - 3)$.
$(3x^2 - 2x + 1) + (2x^2 + 5x - 3)$
$= (3x^2 + 2x^2) + (-2x + 5x) + (1 - 3)$
$= 5x^2 + 3x - 2$

Multiplication

To multiply polynomials, use the distributive property and combine like terms.

Example:

Multiply $(2x - 3)(x + 4)$.
$(2x - 3)(x + 4)$
$= 2x(x + 4) - 3(x + 4)$
$= 2x^2 + 8x - 3x - 12$
$= 2x^2 + 5x - 12$

Division

To divide polynomials, use long division or synthetic division.

Example:

Divide $(3x^3 - 4x^2 + 6x - 5)$ by $(x - 2)$.

Using long division:

$3x^2 - 2x + 3$
x-2 | $3x^3 - 4x^2 + 6x - 5$
$-3x^3 + 6x^2$
_____
$2x^2 + 6x$
$-2x^2 + 4x$
_____
$2x - 5$
$-2x + 4$
_____
-1

The quotient is $3x^2 - 2x + 3$, and the remainder is -1.

Polynomial Equations

A polynomial equation is an equation in which a polynomial is set equal to another polynomial or zero. To solve polynomial equations, use factoring, the quadratic formula (for quadratic equations), or other methods like graphing or using the rational root theorem.

Example:

Solve $x^3 - 5x^2 + 2x + 8 = 0$.

Step 1: Try to factor the polynomial.

$(x^2 - 4)(x - 1) = 0$

Step 2: Set each factor equal to zero and solve.

$x^2 - 4 = 0$ or $x - 1 = 0$

$(x - 2)(x + 2) = 0$ or $x = 1$

$x = 2$, $x = -2$, or $x = 1$

The solutions are $x = 2$, $x = -2$, and $x = 1$.

PRACTICE EXERCISES

Exercise 1:

1. What is the degree of the polynomial $4x^2 - 3x + 5$?

    a) 1
    b) 2
    c) 3
    d) 4

B is the right answer The degree of a polynomial is the highest exponent of its terms. In this polynomial, the highest exponent is 2, making it a quadratic (degree 2) polynomial.

2. What is the value of a if the quadratic equation $(x-3)^2 + 2(x-3) + a = 0$ has a repeated root?

    a) 5
    b) 4
    c) 3
    d) 1

A is the right answer. For a quadratic equation to have a repeated root, the discriminant must be 0. Using the discriminant formula, this gives $b^2 - 4ac = 0$. Substituting the values given, this gives $(2)^2 - 4(1)a = 0$, or $a = 5$.

3. What is the formula used to solve any quadratic equation in the form $ax^2 + bx + c = 0$?

    a) Factorizing
    b) Completing the square

c) Quadratic formula
d) Graphing

C is the right answer. The quadratic formula (-b ± √(b2 - 4ac))/2a provides the exact solutions to any quadratic equation in the form ax2 + bx + c = 0

4. If a quadratic function has the equation y = x^2 - 6x + 8, what is its vertex?

a) (3,8)
b) (3,-8)
c) (-3,1)
d) (3,-1)

D is the right answer. To find the vertex of a quadratic function in the form y = ax^2 + bx + c, we can use the formula:

x = -b / (2a). For this quadratic function: y = x^2 - 6x + 8 where a = 1 b = -6 c = 8. Let's solve it step by step:

x = -b / (2a). x = -(-6) / (2(1)). x = 6 / 2. x = 3.

So the x-coordinate of the vertex is 3. To find the y-coordinate, we plug x = 3 into the original equation:

y = (3)^2 - 6(3) + 8. y = 9 - 18 + 8. y = -1.

Therefore, the vertex of the quadratic function is (3, -1)..

5. What is the sum of the solutions to the quadratic equation 5x^2 - 12x + 6 = 0?

a) 6/5
b) 2
c) 4/5
d) 0

B is the right answer. Using the quadratic formula on 5x2 - 12x + 6 = 0 gives: x = (-(-12) ± √((-12)2 - 4(5)(6))) / 2(5) = 6/5, 6/5. The sum is their sum, which is 2.

6. What is the value of the expression (-3)(-5)(2)?

a) -30
b) 30
c) 15
d) -15

B is the right option. Follow PEMDAS/BODMAS order of operations: -3 × -5 = 15, 15 × 2 = 30.

7. What is the sum of the coefficients of the polynomial 4x^3 - 2x^2 + 7x - 3?

a) 6
b) 4
c) 5
d) 8

A is the right answer. The coefficients are 4, -2, 7, -3. Their sum is 4 - 2 + 7 - 3 = 6.

8. If the quadratic equation (x-a)(x-b) = 0 has equal roots, what is the value of a?

    a) 0
    b) b
    c) a/2
    d) -b

B is the right answer. For a quadratic equation to have equal roots, it means that $a = b$. This is because the roots of the equation (x-a)(x-b) = 0 are x = a and x = b. If a = b, we can rewrite the equation as: (x-a)(x-a) = 0. Expanding this: $x^2 - 2ax + a^2 = 0$. Now, for a quadratic equation in the form $ax^2 + bx + c = 0$ to have equal roots, its discriminant must be zero. The discriminant is given by $b^2 - 4ac$. In our expanded equation ($x^2 - 2ax + a^2 = 0$): a = 1 b = -2a c = a^2. Setting the discriminant to zero: $b^2 - 4ac = 0$ $(-2a)^2 - 4(1)(a^2) = 0$. Simplifying: $4a^2 - 4a^2 = 0$ $0 = 0$.

This equation is true for any value of a. Therefore, we can conclude that: The value of a can be any real number, as long as $a = b$.

9. According to the Fundamental Theorem of Algebra, how many zeroes does a polynomial of degree 5 have?

    a) 3
    b) 5
    c) At most 5
    d) Exactly 5

B is the right answer. By the Fundamental Theorem of Algebra, a polynomial of degree n has n zeros when counted with multiplicity. A degree 5 polynomial can have 5 zeros.

10. Which of the following expressions is NOT a monomial?

    a) 5x
    b) 3x^2y
    c) 4x - 2
    d) x + y

C is the right answer. A monomial is a term with only variables raised to powers and no addition/subtraction between terms. 4x - 2 is not a monomial since it contains subtraction.

Exercise 2

1. What is the degree of the polynomial 4x^3 - 2x + 1?

    a) 1
    b) 2
    c) 3
    d) 4

C is the right option. The degree of a polynomial is the highest power of the variable present. The highest power in the given polynomial is x^3, so the degree is 3.

2. Find the coefficient of x in the polynomial 3x^2 - 5x - 2.

a) -5
b) -2
c) 3
d) 2

A is the right option. To find the coefficient of a term, look at the numeric factor in front of that term. The coefficient of x is -5.

3. Perform: (2x - 3) + (4x + 1)

a) 6x - 2
b) 2x - 4
c) 6x - 1
d) 2x + 4

A is the right option. To add polynomials, combine like terms. The like terms are 2x and 4x, which combine to give 6x. The constant terms -3 and 1 combine to give -2.

4. Factorize completely: x^2 - 9

a) (x - 3)(x + 3)
b) (x + 3)(x - 3)
c) x - 3
d) x + 3

A is the right option. (x - 3)(x + 3) Using the difference of squares factorization, x^2 - 9 = (x - 3)(x + 3).

5. The degree of the product of two polynomials is ___ the sum of the degrees of the factors.

a) Less than
b) Equal to
c) Greater than
d) Divided by

C is the right option. When two polynomials are multiplied, the degree of the product polynomial is equal to the sum of the degrees of the factors.

6. Find the quadratic formula.

a) $x = (-b \pm \sqrt{(b^2 - 4ac)})/2a$
b) $x = (b \pm \sqrt{(b^2 - ac)})/2a$
c) $x = (b \pm \sqrt{(4ab - c)})/2a$
d) $x = (-b \pm \sqrt{(4ac - b^2)})/2a$

A is the right option. This is the correct quadratic formula to solve the general quadratic equation ax^2 + bx + c = 0.

7. The graph of a quadratic equation ax^2 + bx + c = 0 is a/an:

    a) Parabola
    b) Circle
    c) Line
    d) Hyperbola

A is the right option. The graph of a quadratic equation is always a parabola since it is of the form ax^2 + bx + c.

8. Simplify: (x + 1)(x - 1)

    a) x - 1
    b) x^2 - 1
    c) x^2 - x
    d) x + x - 1

B is the right option. Using the foil method, (x + 1)(x - 1) = x^2 - 1.

9. Long division of polynomials _____ the degree of the dividend polynomial.

    a) Increases
    b) Decreases
    c) Does not change
    d) Doubles

B is the right option. Long division of polynomials decreases the degree of the dividend polynomial resulting in a quotient and remainder.

10. Factorize completely: x^2 - 16

    a) (x - 4)(x + 4)
    b) (x - 4)
    c) (x + 4)
    d) x - 4

A is the right option. Using difference of squares, x^2 - 16 = (x - 4)(x + 4).

CHAPTER 8
ADDITIONAL TOPICS IN MATH

In this chapter, we will explore additional mathematical topics that build on concepts from earlier chapters. First, we will review the basics of geometry and trigonometry. This includes revisiting the properties of angles, triangles, circles, polygons, and other geometric shapes. We will examine relationships between side lengths, angles, radii, and more using trigonometric functions like sine, cosine, and tangent. Understanding these fundamentals is crucial for working with more advanced mathematical concepts.

Next, we will introduce the topic of complex numbers. Unlike real numbers that have only a real part, complex numbers have both real and imaginary parts. We will learn how to represent complex numbers on a coordinate plane and using symbolic notation. The chapter will cover how to perform arithmetic operations with complex numbers, such as addition, subtraction, multiplication, and division. We will also explore practical applications of complex numbers in science, engineering, and other fields.

Finally, the chapter includes a selection of practice exercises related to geometry, trigonometry, and complex numbers. Working through these problems will help reinforce the concepts covered and give you an opportunity to apply what you've learned. The skills developed in this chapter will serve as a foundation for more advanced mathematics discussed in later chapters. By the end, you will have gained a deeper understanding of important mathematical building blocks.

GEOMETRY AND TRIGONOMETRY BASICS

Geometry and trigonometry are two closely related branches of mathematics that deal with measurements and relationships in two-dimensional and three-dimensional space. Both subjects begin with basic topics like points, lines, angles, and shapes, and build up to more advanced concepts involving algebraic formulas and problem solving. This comprehensive guide will explore the core principles and applications of geometry and trigonometry in an easy to understand manner.

Geometry Basics

Geometry refers to the study of shapes, spatial relationships, and properties of points, lines, surfaces, and solids. Some key fundamental concepts in geometry include:

Points:
A point is a specific location or place that has no size. Points are represented by a dot in geometry diagrams.

Lines:
A line extends indefinitely in both directions and has no thickness. It contains an infinite number of points. Lines are represented by a straight path on diagrams.

Line Segments:

A line segment connects two distinct points and has defined endpoints. It is represented by a straight arrow symbolized by two points.

Rays:
A ray has one endpoint and extends indefinitely in one direction. It contains its endpoint and all points along its path away from that point. A ray is symbolized by an arrow pointing away from its endpoint.

Angles:
An angle is formed by two rays that share a common endpoint, known as the vertex. Basic angle types include acute, obtuse, right, straight, reflex, zero, and complete/full angles. Angles are measured in degrees.

Shapes:
Some basic geometric shapes studied include points, lines, line segments, rays, polygons (triangles, quadrilaterals, pentagons, etc.), circles, ellipses, parabolas, and spheres.

Parallel and Perpendicular Lines:

Parallel lines lie in the same plane and never intersect. Perpendicular lines intersect to form right angles.

Quadrilaterals:
Four-sided polygons include squares, rectangles, parallelograms, trapezoids, and kites. Properties differ based on side lengths, angles, and other factors.

Circles:
A circle consists of all points equidistant from a central point called the center. Key parts are the radius, diameter, chord, arc, and circumference.

Area and Perimeter:
The area of a shape represents the amount of space it encloses, measured in standard units like square inches or centimeters. Perimeter is the distance around the outer edge of a shape.

Trigonometric Functions

Trigonometry utilizes specific geometric relationships involving angles and ratios of sides in triangles. The six main trigonometric functions are:

Sine:
The ratio of the length of the side opposite an angle to the length of the hypotenuse. Written as sin(angle).

Cosine:
The ratio of the length of the side adjacent to an angle to the hypotenuse. Written as cos(angle).

Tangent:
The ratio of the length of the opposite side to the adjacent side for a given angle. Written as tan(angle).

Cosecant:

The ratio of the hypotenuse to the opposite side. Csc(angle).

Secant:

The ratio of the hypotenuse to the adjacent side. Sec(angle).

Cotangent:
The ratio of the adjacent side to the opposite side. Cot(angle).

The trig functions are commonly used to solve problems relating unknown lengths and angles based on a central right triangle formed within a larger diagram or context. Trig tables and calculators provide the exact values of these ratios for standard angles.

COMPLEX NUMBERS

Complex numbers are a mathematical extension of real numbers. They incorporate an imaginary unit, denoted by "i", where i^2 equals negative one (-1). This allows complex numbers to represent solutions for polynomial equations that wouldn't have solutions using only real numbers. Because of this unique property, complex numbers find applications in various fields like electrical engineering, quantum physics, and beyond.

Representation

Complex numbers can be represented in several ways:

Cartesian Form:

This uses the standard form $a + bi$, where a and b are real numbers and $i = \sqrt{-1}$.

For example, 3 + 2i represents the complex number with a real part of 3 and imaginary part of 2.

Polar Form: This expresses a complex number as $r(\cos\theta + i\sin\theta)$, where r is the absolute value (distance from origin) and θ is the angle measured counterclockwise from the positive real axis. **For example**, $5(\cos 60° + i\sin 60°) = 5(1/2 + i\sqrt{3}/2)$.

Exponential Form: Complex numbers can also be written as $re^{i\theta}$, utilizing Euler's famous formula $e^{i\theta} = \cos\theta + i\sin\theta$. This relates imaginary exponents to trigonometric functions.

Operations with Complex Numbers

Basic arithmetic operations can be carried out on complex numbers by treating real and imaginary parts separately:

Addition: $(a + bi) + (c + di) = (a + c) + (b + d)i$

Subtraction: $(a + bi) - (c + di) = (a - c) + (b - d)i$

Multiplication: $(a + bi)(c + di) = (ac - bd) + (ad + bc)i$

Division: $(a + bi)/(c + di) = (ac + bd)/(c2 + d2) + (bc - ad)/(c2 + d2)i$

Conjugation: The conjugate of $(a + bi)$ is $(a - bi)$. It is obtained by changing the sign of the imaginary part.

Magnitude: $|a + bi| = \sqrt{a^2 + b^2}$, the distance from the origin to the complex number point.

Complex Functions

Many common functions, like exponential, logarithmic, trigonometric, can be extended to complex numbers. Key properties include:

Exponential: $e^{\wedge}(a+bi) = e^{\wedge}a(\cos(b) + i\sin(b))$

Logarithm: If $z = re^{i\theta}$, then $\ln(z) = \ln(r) + i\theta$

Trigonometric: $\sin(a+bi)$, $\cos(a+bi)$, $\tan(a+bi)$ are periodic, producing spirals.

Inverse Trig: arcsin, arccos, arctan have multiple values due to trig branches.

Square Root: $\sqrt{(a + bi)} = \sqrt{(\sqrt{(a^2+b^2)}/2)}(1 + i)$ if $a,b \geq 0$

Complex Numbers and Algebraic Equations

By treating variables as complex numbers, polynomials with real coefficients can have complex number solutions even when no real number solution exists. Every polynomial equation of degree n has exactly n complex number solutions when counted with multiplicity.

For example, the quadratic equation $x^{\wedge}2 + 1 = 0$ has the solutions $x = \pm i$. Cubic and higher-degree equations may have multiple complex solutions as well through formulas like Cardano's method.

Geometry and Complex Numbers

Complex numbers allow geometric representations and interpretations:

- Points in the complex plane correspond 1-1 with the complex numbers themselves.
- Complex functions graph as curves in this plane, like the unit circle for complex exponential and trig functions.
- Rotations, stretches and other transformations map to complex multiplications and fractions.
- Mandelbrot and Julia sets showcase the geometry arising from iterated complex functions.

PRACTICE EXERCISES

Exercise 1

1.What is the value of i^2?

    a) 1
    b) -1

c) 2i

d) i

B is the correct option. By definition, i^2 = -1

2. Which of the following allows finding all solutions to a polynomial equation?

a) Real numbers

b) Integers

c) Complex numbers

d) Rational numbers

C is the correct option. Complex numbers allow all polynomial equations to have as many solutions as their degree.

3. What is the Cartesian form of the complex number with magnitude 3 and argument π/4?

a) 3 + i√2

b) √2 + i

c) 3(1/√2 + i 1/√2)

d) √2 - i

C is the correct option. This has r=3, θ=π/4. The Cartesian form of a complex number is a + bi, where a is the real part and b is the imaginary part.

We're given the polar form information:

Magnitude (r) = 3

Argument (θ) = π/4

To convert from polar to Cartesian form, we use these formulas:

a = r * cos(θ)

b = r * sin(θ)

Let's calculate a: a = 3 * cos(π/4)

cos(π/4) = 1/√2 ≈ 0.7071

a = 3 * (1/√2) = 3/√2 ≈ 2.1213

Now let's calculate b: b = 3 * sin(π/4)

sin(π/4) = 1/√2 ≈ 0.7071

b = 3 * (1/√2) = 3/√2 ≈ 2.1213

Therefore, our complex number in Cartesian form is: (3/√2) + (3/√2)i = 3(1/√2 + i 1/√2)

4. If z = 5 + 3i, then the conjugate of z is:

a) 5 - 3i

b) 3 + 5i

c) 5i - 3
d) 3i - 5

A is the correct option. The conjugate is obtained by changing the sign of the imaginary part.

5. What is the perimeter of an equilateral triangle with side 7 cm?

a) 14cm
b) 21cm
c) 28cm
d) 35cm

B is the correct option. An equilateral triangle has all sides equal, and perimeter is 3 times the side length.

6. What is the positive angle less than 360° that is coterminal with an angle of 425°?

a) 25°
b) 65°
c) 155°
d) 295°

B is the correct option. We know that coterminal angles differ by multiples of 360°. To find the coterminal angle less than 360°, we need to subtract 360° from 425° as many times as necessary until we get an angle less than 360°. 425° - 360° = 65°

7. The arc length of a sector with central angle 30° in a circle of radius 5 cm is:

a) π/6 cm
b) 1.5π cm
c) 3 cm
d) 5π/6 cm

D is the right option. The formula for arc length (s) is: s = (θ/360°) * 2πr where θ is the central angle in degrees, and r is the radius. We're given: θ = 30° r = 5 cm. Let's substitute these into our formula: s = (30/360) * 2π * 5. Simplify: s = (1/12) * 2π * 5 s = (5/6)π

8. What is the tangent of 45°?

a) 1
b) √2
c) 2
d) 1/√2

A is the correct option. The tangent of 45° is 1.

9. Find the area of a rhombus with diagonal 14cm and 30cm.

a) 120 cm^2
b) 140 cm^2
c) 210 cm^2

d) 280 cm^2

C is the right option. Area = 1/2 × diagonal1 × diagonal2

10. Which of the following can be used to represent the cube root of -8?

a) 1+i√3
b) -2
c) 1-i√3
d) all of them

D is the right option. To find the complex cube roots, we use the formula:

z = r^(1/3) * (cos((θ + 2πk)/3) + i*sin((θ + 2πk)/3))

Where:

- r is the magnitude of the number (in this case, 8)
- θ is the argument of the number (in this case, π radians or 180°)
- k = 0, 1, 2 for the three roots

Plugging in these values:

For k = 0: 2 * (cos(π/3) + isin(π/3)) = 2 * (1/2 + i(√3/2)) = 1 + i√3

For k = 1: 2 * (cos(π) + i*sin(π)) = 2 * (-1 + 0i) = -2

For k = 2: 2 * (cos(5π/3) + isin(5π/3)) = 2 * (1/2 - i(√3/2)) = 1 - i√3

These are the three complex cube roots of -8.

Exercise 2

1. What is the solution set of the equation z^2 = i?

a) {(√2/2) + (√2/2)i, -(√2/2) - (√2/2)i}
b) {±1, ±i}
c) {(1/√2) + (1/√2)i, -(1/√2) - (1/√2)i}
d) {-1, i}

A is the correct option. First, let's express i in polar form: i = 1 * cis(π/2). To find the square roots, we use the formula: z = r^(1/n) * cis((θ + 2πk) / n). where r is the magnitude, θ is the argument, n is the root (in this case 2), and k = 0, 1, ..., n-1

Plugging in our values: r = 1, θ = π/2, n = 2, k = 0, 1, For k = 0: z_1 = 1^(1/2) * cis((π/2 + 2π*0) / 2) = cis(π/4) = (√2/2) + (√2/2)i

For k = 1: z_2 = 1^(1/2) * cis((π/2 + 2π*1) / 2) = cis(5π/4) = -(√2/2) - (√2/2)i

2. If sin(A) = 3/5, what is the cosine of angle A?

a) ±4/5

b) ±12/25
c) ±3/5
d) -3/5 Using the Pythagorean identity, cos^2(A) + sin^2(A) = 1.

A is the correct option. Using the Pythagorean identity, cos^2(A) + sin^2(A) = 1.

3. What is the perimeter of a square with diagonal 24 cm?

a) 24√2 cm
b) 48/√2 cm
c) √2 cm
d) 12√2 cm

B is the right option. In a square, the diagonal forms the hypotenuse of a right triangle where the other two sides are the sides of the square. If we call the side length of the square s, we can use the Pythagorean theorem: s² + s² = 24². Simplify: 2s² = 24², 2s² = 576. Solve for s: s² = 576 / 2 = 288, s = √288. Simplify √288: √288 = √(16 * 18) = 4√18 = 4 * 3√2 = 12√2. So the side length of the square is 12√2 cm. The perimeter of a square is 4 times its side length: Perimeter = 4 * 12√2 = 48√2 cm

4. What is the complex number represented by the point (4, -3) in the complex plane?

a) 4 - 3i
b) -3 + 4i
c) 3 - 4i
d) -4 + 3i

A is the correct option. The point's x-coordinate is the real part and y is the imaginary part.

5. The distance between two complex numbers z1 and z2 is given by:

a) |z1 - z2|
b) |z1| - |z2|
c) |z1| + |z2|
d) z1z2

A is the correct option. Distance formula |z1 - z2| gives magnitude of difference.

6. Simplify: (2+i)(3-2i)

a) 5 - 3i
b) 1 + 5i
c) 8 - i
d) 8 + i

C is the correct option. Distribute and combine like terms.

7. In △ABC, sinA = 3/5, cosA = 4/5. The value of tanA is:

a) 3/4
b) 9/25
c) 4/3
d) 3/5

A is the correct option. Using the definitions tanA = sinA/cosA.

8. The ratio of circumference to diameter of a circle is approximately:

a) π/4
b) π/3
c) π
d) 3π

A is the correct option. The ratio is π.

9. If one interior angle of a regular polygon is 150°, the number of sides is:

c) 8 For a regular polygon, interior angle sum is (n-2)180. So 150(n-2)=1440 gives n=8.
a) 5
b) 6
c) 8
d) 10

A is the correct option. For a regular polygon, interior angle sum is (n-2)180. So 150(n-2)=1440 gives n=8.

10. Evaluate i^1000 + i^-1000

a) 0
b) 1
c) -1
d) i

A is the correct option. i^1000 and i^-1000 cancel each other out as complex powers of i repeat every 4 units.

SUBMIT A REVIEW

Did these pages help, inspire, or bring you value in any way? If so, we'd love to hear your thoughts through an honest review on Amazon. Your feedback is incredibly valuable to us!

It's very simple and only takes a few minutes:

1. Go to the "My Orders" page on Amazon and search the book.
2. Select "Write a product review".
3. Select a Star Rating.
4. Optionally, add text, photos, or videos and select Submit.

PART IV

TEST-TAKING STRATEGIES AND TIPS

CHAPTER 9
GENERAL TEST-TAKING STRATEGIES

Effective time management, handling difficult questions smartly, and reducing anxiety on test day are important for showing your full knowledge and skills on exams. Preparing well is essential for success.

Creating a testing schedule helps you keep track of time during the exam. Spend more time on question types or topics you find hard and leave time at the end to review any flagged questions. If you're running out of time, skip long calculations and focus on questions you can answer quickly and confidently.

When you face a tough question, take a deep breath, and read it carefully to understand what it's asking. Eliminate answers that don't make sense, then make an educated guess instead of leaving it blank. Mark difficult questions for review later so you can focus on easier ones. Staying positive helps you not get stuck on one problem.

Relaxing before the test through deep breathing can reduce stress, helping your mind work better. Get organized the night before by visualizing success and preparing all needed materials. During the test, breathe steadily to stay calm and focus on one question at a time. Read and understand the directions carefully at the beginning to avoid unnecessary mistakes. If you feel overwhelmed, pause and re-focus your thoughts.

TIME MANAGEMENT DURING THE EXAM

Effective time management is essential for success on the SAT®, as the exam is timed and can be challenging to complete in the allotted time. Here are some strategies to help you manage your time effectively:

1. Know the test structure and timing: Familiarize yourself with the number of sections, the types of questions in each section, and the time allotted for each section. This will help you pace yourself appropriately and avoid spending too much time on any one question or section.
2. Practice with timed sections: When preparing for the SAT®, take full-length practice tests under timed conditions to simulate the actual test experience. This will help you develop a sense of pacing and identify areas where you may need to speed up or slow down.
3. Answer easy questions first: When you encounter a question that seems easy or straightforward, answer it first. This will help you build momentum and confidence, and it will ensure that you don't miss out on points for questions you could have answered correctly.
4. Skip difficult questions: If you encounter a question that seems particularly challenging or time-consuming, skip it and move on to the next question. You can always come back to it later if you have time remaining. It's better to complete as many questions as possible than to get stuck on one difficult question and run out of time.
5. Use process of elimination: If you're unsure of the correct answer to a question, use the process of elimination to narrow down your choices. Eliminate any answer choices that are clearly incorrect, and then make an educated guess from the remaining options. This strategy can help you save time and increase your chances of selecting the correct answer.
6. Keep track of time: During the exam, keep an eye on the clock and be aware of how much time you have left in each section. If you find yourself falling behind, try to pick up the pace without sacrificing accuracy. If you're ahead of schedule, use the extra time to double-check your answers or attempt any skipped questions.

Let's say you have 60 minutes to complete a 50-question section. A good pacing strategy would be to aim to complete the first 25 questions in about 25-30 minutes, leaving yourself 30-35 minutes for the remaining 25 questions. This gives you a little extra time to tackle more challenging questions or review your answers.

HANDLING DIFFICULT QUESTIONS

Even with thorough preparation, you may encounter questions on the SAT® that seem particularly challenging. Here are some strategies for handling difficult questions:

1. Read the question carefully: Make sure you understand what the question is asking. Read it slowly and carefully, and pay attention to key words and phrases that provide clues to the correct answer.
2. Break it down: If the question seems overwhelming, try breaking it down into smaller, more manageable parts. Identify the given information, the unknown, and any relevant concepts or formulas that may help you solve the problem.
3. Visualize the problem: If applicable, try to visualize the problem by sketching a diagram, picture, or graph. This can help you better understand the relationship between the given information and the question being asked.
4. Use educated guessing: If you're unable to solve the problem or eliminate any answer choices, make an educated guess. Look for answer choices that seem plausible or consistent with the given information and avoid any choices that are clearly incorrect or contradictory.
5. Move on: If you've spent a reasonable amount of time on a difficult question and still can't solve it, move on to the next question. It's better to attempt as many questions as possible than to get stuck on one challenging problem and risk running out of time.

Consider a challenging word problem in the Math section. First, read the question carefully to identify the key information and the question being asked. Then, try to break down the problem into smaller steps, visualizing the situation if helpful. If you're still unsure, use educated guessing to eliminate any answer choices that seem implausible or inconsistent with the given information. Finally, if you've spent a few minutes on the problem without making progress, move on to the next question to manage your time effectively.

REDUCING TEST-DAY ANXIETY

Test-day anxiety is a common experience for many students, but there are several strategies you can use to reduce stress and maintain a positive mindset during the exam:

1. Prepare thoroughly: One of the best ways to reduce test-day anxiety is to prepare thoroughly in the weeks and months leading up to the exam. Take practice tests, review key concepts, and focus on areas where you need improvement. The more prepared you feel, the more confident and less anxious you'll be on test day.
2. Get a good night's sleep: Aim to get a full 8 hours of sleep the night before the exam. Being well-rested will help you feel more alert, focused, and capable of performing your best.
3. Eat a healthy breakfast: On the morning of the test, eat a nutritious breakfast that will provide you with sustained energy throughout the exam. Avoid heavy, greasy

foods that may make you feel sluggish, and limit your caffeine intake to avoid jitters or crashes.

4. Arrive early: Plan to arrive at the test center early to allow yourself plenty of time to check in, find your room, and get settled. Rushing or arriving late can increase your stress levels and negatively impact your performance.

5. Practice relaxation techniques: During the exam, if you find yourself feeling anxious or overwhelmed, take a moment to practice relaxation techniques such as deep breathing, progressive muscle relaxation, or positive self-talk. These techniques can help you calm down, refocus, and approach the remaining questions with a clearer mind.

If you find yourself feeling anxious during the exam, try taking a few deep breaths. Inhale slowly through your nose for a count of four, hold your breath for a count of four, then exhale slowly through your mouth for a count of four. Repeat this process a few times until you feel more relaxed and centered.

MAINTAINING ENDURANCE AND FOCUS

The SAT® is a long and mentally demanding exam, and it's essential to maintain your endurance and focus throughout the test. Here are some tips for staying sharp and avoiding burnout:

1. Take breaks: During the short breaks between sections, take a moment to stretch, relax, and clear your mind. Use this time to give your brain a brief rest before diving into the next section.

2. Stay hydrated: Bring a water bottle with you to the test center and take sips throughout the exam to stay hydrated. Dehydration can lead to fatigue, headaches, and decreased mental performance.

3. Maintain good posture: Sit up straight and avoid slouching or hunching over your desk. Good posture can help you stay alert and focused, while poor posture can lead to fatigue and decreased concentration.

4. Avoid overthinking: If you find yourself getting stuck on a particular question or second-guessing your answers, try to avoid overthinking. Trust your instincts and the preparation you've done, and move on to the next question to maintain your momentum.

5. Stay motivated: Remember why you're taking the SAT® and what you hope to achieve. Keep your goals and aspirations in mind throughout the exam, and use them as motivation to stay focused and give your best effort.

During the short break between sections, stand up, stretch your arms and legs, and take a few deep breaths. Close your eyes and visualize yourself successfully completing the next section, maintaining your focus and confidence. Take a sip of water, and then return to your seat feeling refreshed and ready to tackle the remaining questions.

CHAPTER 10
SECTION-SPECIFIC STRATEGIES

Different parts of the SAT® require different approaches. This chapter talks about specific strategies for the Reading, Writing and Language, and Math sections. Instead of using the same strategy for everything, it's better to learn techniques that fit each section's style. The next parts explain how to confidently handle tough reading passages, tricky sentence corrections, and hard math problems. From breaking down complex reading questions to making math problems simpler, knowing how to use your strengths for each part helps you show that you're good at many skills. Learning these tailored strategies helps you feel ready for any type of question. By studying these techniques closely, you'll be ready to do your best in all parts of the SAT®.

STRATEGIES FOR THE READING SECTION

The Reading section of the SAT® assesses your comprehension and reasoning skills across a range of passages, including literature, social studies, and science. Here are some strategies to help you navigate this section effectively:

1. Skim the passage first: Before diving into the questions, take a moment to skim the passage, paying attention to the main idea, key terms, and overall structure. This will give you a general understanding of the content and make it easier to locate relevant information when answering questions.
2. Read actively: As you read the passage more closely, engage with the text by underlining key phrases, making brief notes in the margins, and asking yourself questions about the main ideas and the author's purpose. Active reading will help you stay focused and retain important information.
3. Answer questions strategically: When tackling the questions, start with the ones that seem easiest or most straightforward. This will help you build momentum and avoid getting stuck on challenging questions early on. If a question seems difficult or time-consuming, skip it and come back to it later if time allows.
4. Use process of elimination: For questions with multiple answer choices, use the process of elimination to narrow down your options. Eliminate any choices that are clearly incorrect or contradictory to the information in the passage, and then select the best answer from the remaining choices.
5. Refer back to the passage: Many questions will require you to refer back to specific parts of the passage to find the correct answer. Don't be afraid to re-read relevant sections or use the information you underlined or noted during your initial reading.

Consider a question that asks about the main idea of a passage. First, refer back to your initial skim and any notes you made about the overall structure and key points. Then, read through the answer choices, eliminating any that are too narrow, too broad, or unsupported by the passage. Finally, select the choice that best captures the central idea conveyed throughout the text.

STRATEGIES FOR THE WRITING AND LANGUAGE SECTION

The Writing and Language section of the SAT® tests your ability to revise and edit passages for clarity, coherence, and adherence to standard English conventions. Here are some strategies to help you approach this section effectively:

1. Read the passage carefully: Before answering any questions, read through the entire passage to get a sense of its overall meaning and structure. Pay attention to the main idea, tone, and transitions between sentences and paragraphs.

2. Identify the underlined portions: Most questions in this section will refer to specific underlined portions of the passage. Identify these portions and read them in context to determine if any revisions are necessary.

3. Consider the options: For each question, carefully read through all of the answer choices, considering how each one would affect the meaning, clarity, or grammatical correctness of the passage. Eliminate any choices that are clearly incorrect or inconsistent with the rest of the text.

4. Look for common errors: Be on the lookout for common writing and language errors, such as subject-verb agreement, pronoun-antecedent agreement, parallel structure, and misplaced modifiers. Identifying these errors can help you quickly eliminate incorrect answer choices.

5. Read the revised sentence: Before selecting your final answer, read the sentence or paragraph with your chosen revision in place to ensure that it sounds correct and fits logically with the rest of the passage.

Consider a question that asks you to choose the best transition word or phrase to connect two sentences. Read the sentences before and after the underlined portion to understand the relationship between the ideas being expressed. Then, consider each answer choice and how it would affect the logical flow of the passage. Eliminate any choices that create awkward or illogical transitions, and select the one that best clarifies the connection between the sentences.

STRATEGIES FOR THE MATH SECTION

The Math section of the SAT® assesses your problem-solving skills and understanding of key mathematical concepts, including algebra, geometry, and data analysis. Here are some strategies to help you approach this section effectively:

1. Read the question carefully: Make sure you understand what each question is asking and what information is provided. Identify the key elements of the problem, such as the given values and the unknown you need to solve for.

2. Identify relevant concepts: Determine which mathematical concepts or formulas are needed to solve the problem. Recall any relevant definitions, properties, or equations that you've learned during your preparation.

3. Solve step-by-step: Break the problem down into smaller, more manageable steps. Show your work clearly, and use proper notation and units as needed. Avoid taking mental shortcuts or making assumptions, as this can lead to errors.

4. Double-check your work: Before moving on to the next question, take a moment to review your solution and ensure that it makes sense and answers the question being asked. Check for any arithmetic errors or missed steps and verify that your answer is in the correct form and within the given range, if applicable.

5. Use estimation: If a question involves complex calculations or gives answer choices that are far apart, use estimation to quickly eliminate any choices that are clearly incorrect. This can save you time and help you narrow down your options.

Consider a question that asks you to solve a system of linear equations. First, read the question carefully to identify the given equations and any additional information provided. Then, determine the best method for solving the system (e.g., substitution, elimination, or graphing), and proceed step-by-step to isolate the variables and find the solution. Finally, double-check your work by plugging the solution back into the original equations to verify that it satisfies both conditions.

EFFICIENT PROBLEM SOLVING

Across all sections of the SAT®, efficient problem solving is key to maximizing your performance and avoiding common pitfalls. Here are some general tips for approaching problems efficiently:

1. Prioritize: Start with the questions or problems that seem easiest or most straightforward and work your way up to the more challenging ones. This will help you build confidence and momentum and ensure that you don't miss out on points for questions you could have answered correctly.
2. Manage your time: Keep track of the time you're spending on each section and avoid getting bogged down on any one question or problem. If you find yourself stuck, make an educated guess, and move on, rather than wasting valuable time.
3. Use your resources: Take advantage of any resources provided on the test, such as formulas, diagrams, or reference information. Don't waste time trying to memorize information that's readily available to you.
4. Check your work: Whenever possible, take a moment to review your answers and check for any errors or inconsistencies. This can help you catch mistakes and avoid losing points for careless errors.

In the Math section, if you encounter a question that seems particularly challenging or time-consuming, don't hesitate to skip it and move on to the next one. You can always come back to it later if time allows, but it's better to complete as many questions as possible than to get stuck on one difficult problem and risk running out of time.

SUBMIT A REVIEW

Did these pages help, inspire, or bring you value in any way? If so, we'd love to hear your thoughts through an honest review on Amazon. Your feedback is incredibly valuable to us!

It's very simple and only takes a few minutes:

1. Go to the "My Orders" page on Amazon and search the book.
2. Select "Write a product review".
3. Select a Star Rating.
4. Optionally, add text, photos, or videos and select Submit.

PART V

PRACTICE TESTS AND SOLUTIONS

CHAPTER 11
FULL-LENGTH PRACTICE TEST

PRACTICE TEST #1

Reading and Writing test – Module 1
32 Minutes, 27 Questions
Direction

The questions in this section address a number of important reading and writing skills. Each question includes one or more passages, which may include a table or graph. Read each passage and question carefully, and then choose the best answer to the question based on the passage(s). All questions in this section are multiple-choice with four answer choices. Each question has a single best answer.

1

The poet Maya Angelou is known for her powerful and evocative verses. Her poetry often _____ themes of identity, resilience, and the human experience.

Which choice completes the text with the most logical and precise word or phrase?

    A) Trivializes
    B) Explores
    C) Ignores
    D) Simplifies

2

The following text is from Ralph Ellison's 1952 novel "Invisible Man."

The protagonist navigates a society that refuses to see him, struggling with issues of identity and invisibility.

A) Which choice best describes the function of the underlined sentence in the text as a whole?
B) It introduces a major theme of the novel.
C) It describes the setting of the story.
D) It provides background information about the protagonist.
E) It explains the plot of the novel.

3

In 2017, historian Dr. Laura Green published a book on the cultural impact of the Renaissance. She argued that the period's emphasis on humanism and individualism _____ modern Western thought.

Which choice completes the text with the most logical and precise word or phrase?

A) hindered
B) ignored
C) shaped
D) complicated

4

The scientist Nikola Tesla is best known for his contributions to the development of alternating current (AC) electricity. His innovative ideas and inventions _____ the field of electrical engineering.

Which choice completes the text with the most logical and precise word or phrase?

A) transformed
B) halted
C) neglected
D) overshadowed

5

The following text is from Leo Tolstoy's 1877 novel "Anna Karenina."

Anna reflects on her life choices and the consequences of her actions. Her internal struggle reveals the complexities of her emotions and desires.

Which choice best describes the function of the underlined sentence in the text as a whole?
A) It describes Anna's external circumstances.
B) It provides insight into Anna's character development.
C) It introduces a new plot point.
D) It summarizes the central conflict of the novel.

6

In 2016, Dr. Sam Parker conducted a study on the effects of urbanization on bird populations. He discovered that some bird species have _____ their nesting habits to thrive in city environments.

Which choice completes the text with the most logical and precise word or phrase?

    A) abandoned
    B) adapted
    C) isolated
    D) worsened

7

The author J.K. Rowling is known for her Harry Potter series, which has _____ the imaginations of readers worldwide with its magical world and compelling characters.

Which choice completes the text with the most logical and precise word or phrase?

    A) confused
    B) dampened
    C) captured
    D) overlooked

8

The following text is from Ernest Hemingway's 1952 novella "The Old Man and the Sea."

Santiago, an old fisherman, battles a giant marlin far out in the Gulf Stream. The struggle between the man and the fish highlights themes of perseverance and dignity.

    Which choice best describes the function of the underlined sentence in the text as a whole?
    A) It introduces the main conflict of the story.
    B) It provides background information about Santiago.
    C) It describes the setting of the story.
    D) It explains the significance of the marlin.

9

In 2020, Dr. Lisa Wong conducted a study on the benefits of early childhood education. Her research indicated that children who attend preschool programs _____ better academic and social outcomes later in life.

Which choice completes the text with the most logical and precise word or phrase?

    A) experience
    B) neglect
    C) hinder
    D) confuse

10

The musician Miles Davis is celebrated for his contributions to jazz music. His innovative approach and willingness to _____ traditional boundaries have left a lasting impact on the genre.

Which choice completes the text with the most logical and precise word or phrase?

    A) adhere to
    B) redefine
    C) simplify
    D) preserve

11

As the first Indigenous leader of the modern era, Chief Nako became one of the most _____ figures in his nation's history: during his leadership (2000–2015), Chief Nako strengthened the central government and advocated for environmental preservation.

Which choice completes the text with the most logical and precise word or phrase?

    A) controversial
    B) prominent
    C) secretive
    D) ordinary

12

Due to their often abstract themes, unconventional syntax, and complex imagery, many of Emma Brown's poems can be quite challenging to _____ and thus are the subject of much debate among literary critics.

Which choice completes the text with the most logical and precise word or phrase?

    A) understand
    B) ignore
    C) replicate
    D) summarize

13

The sudden appearance and rapid diversification of animal life in the fossil record about 540 million years ago is referred to as the Cambrian explosion. Some scientists suggest that this _____ change could be due to the development of hard body parts that are more likely to fossilize.

Which choice completes the text with the most logical and precise word or phrase?

    A) gradual
    B) steady

C) abrupt
D) slow

14

During a 2015 archaeological excavation in Greece, researchers uncovered the remains of a woman buried with valuable artifacts from the Early Bronze Age. This discovery might lead scholars, who have long believed Bronze Age societies were male-dominated, to _____ that women may have also held significant power.

Which choice completes the text with the most logical and precise word or phrase?

A) insist
B) accept
C) refute
D) ignore

15

In some species of deep-sea fish, individuals develop an additional swim bladder—a seemingly unnecessary formation. Given its prevalence among fish that dive to great depths, some researchers hypothesize that its role isn't _____; rather, the additional swim bladder may support diving adaptations.

Which choice completes the text with the most logical and precise word or phrase?

A) decorative
B) passive
C) critical
D) random

16

According to an economist, state taxes are _____ other factors when considering an interstate move. Even significant differences in state taxation have minimal effect on most people's decisions, while differences in job opportunities, housing availability, and climate are strong influences.

Which choice completes the text with the most logical and precise word or phrase?

A) aligned with
B) secondary to
C) overshadowed by
D) unrelated to

17

The author's theory about the relationship between Neanderthals and modern humans is _____ because it does not consider recent archaeological discoveries. To be convincing, the argument must address new findings such as the latest Denisovan specimens and Homo longi fossils.

Which choice completes the text with the most logical and precise word or phrase?

A) groundbreaking
B) flawed
C) insightful
D) comprehensive

18

The following text is from a poem by a contemporary author.

Go forth, my child,

With dreams that know no bounds!
Great adventures, yet unknown,
Await
Your embrace.
I cannot walk with you,
My journey is complete,
But life is calling you!

Which choice best states the main purpose of the text?

A) To encourage a child to embrace the experiences life will offer
B) To suggest that raising a child involves many struggles
C) To warn a child that he will face many challenges throughout his life
D) To express hope that a child will have the same accomplishments as his parent did

19

The following text is adapted from a memoir by a rural farmer. The author describes the traditional methods used by his community to collect honey.

The beekeepers began to inspect the hives—moving slowly among them, smoker in hand, and puffing smoke gently to calm the bees. The hives, like people, have their unique traits; some were quick to yield their honey, while others were more resistant. Now, wooden frames were carefully removed, and honeycombs were cut and placed into containers. From these combs—initially trickling, then flowing steadily—the golden honey dripped into the jars.

Which choice best describes the function of the underlined sentence in the text as a whole?

A) It demonstrates how human behavior can be influenced by the natural environment.
B) It elaborates on an aspect of the hives that the beekeepers evaluate.
C) It portrays the range of personality traits displayed by the beekeepers as they work.
D) It foregrounds the beneficial relationship between humans and bees.

20

Text 1 Marine biologists have long puzzled over how numerous species of tiny plankton can coexist in the ocean's surface waters while competing for the same resources. According to conventional theories, one species should eventually dominate. So why do so many species persist? Despite various theories, a satisfactory explanation remains elusive.

Text 2 Marine biologist Dr. Lila Johnson and her team have linked plankton diversity to their minute size. These organisms, being so small, are spaced relatively far apart in ocean water and experience it as a dense medium. This separation makes it difficult for them to interact and compete directly. Thus, Johnson's team suggests that direct competition among plankton is less frequent than previously assumed.

Based on the texts, how would Johnson and her team (Text 2) most likely respond to the "conventional theories" discussed in Text 1?

A) By arguing that the theories are based on a misunderstanding of plankton competition
B) By asserting that they fail to recognize that nutrient replenishment prevents competition among plankton species
C) By suggesting that their own findings clarify how plankton avoid direct competition
D) By recommending more research on how plankton size influences competition

21

In 2016, Amelia Quon and her team at a space research organization set out to design a drone capable of flying on Titan, one of Saturn's moons. Due to Titan's dense atmosphere, a standard drone designed for Earth would not generate enough lift. For several years, Quon's team tested various designs in a chamber simulating Titan's atmospheric condition. The final design features longer, faster-rotating blades, enabling the drone to fly in Titan's thick air.

According to the text, why would a drone built for Earth be unable to fly on Titan?

A) Because Titan's atmosphere is much denser than Earth's
B) Because the blades of drones built for Earth are too small to work on Titan
C) Because Titan's gravity is much weaker than Earth's
D) Because drones built for Earth are not durable enough for Titan's conditions

22

In 2020, Dr. Jamie Carter studied the impact of deforestation on tropical bird species. He found that as forests were cleared, bird populations _____ significantly.

Which choice completes the text with the most logical and precise word or phrase?

A) increased
B) stabilized

C) declined
D) diversified

23

"In recent years, electric scooters have surged in popularity as an eco-friendly alternative to traditional modes of transportation. While they offer a convenient and efficient means of travel, particularly in urban areas, their rapid integration into cityscapes has sparked debates over safety regulations and infrastructure adaptation."

Which choice best states the main idea of the passage?

A) Electric scooters are the most eco-friendly mode of transportation.
B) The popularity of electric scooters has led to discussions about safety and infrastructure.
C) Urban areas are well-adapted to the influx of electric scooters.
D) Traditional transportation methods are being replaced by electric scooters.

24

"After analyzing over 2,000 photographs of Earth taken from space, scientists discovered that urban areas emit significantly more artificial light than previously estimated. This increased brightness not only disrupts the natural behaviors of nocturnal animals but also contributes to energy wastage and increased greenhouse gas emissions."

Which choice most effectively summarizes the passage?

A) Scientists have taken numerous photographs of Earth from space.
B) Artificial light from urban areas disrupts nocturnal animals.
C) Urban areas emit more artificial light than estimated, affecting animals and the environment.
D) Increased brightness in urban areas is due to energy wastage.

25

"The advent of digital media has revolutionized the way people consume news. Traditional newspapers, once the primary source of information, have seen a decline in circulation as readers increasingly turn to online platforms for instant updates. This shift has compelled news organizations to adapt by enhancing their digital presence and leveraging social media to engage with audiences."

What is the author's primary purpose in the passage?

A) To criticize the decline of traditional newspapers.
B) To explain the impact of digital media on news consumption.
C) To promote the use of social media for news updates.
D) To suggest that traditional newspapers should stop printing.

26

"Many studies have highlighted the benefits of physical activity on mental health. Regular exercise has been shown to reduce symptoms of anxiety and depression, improve mood, and boost overall cognitive function. Moreover, engaging in physical activities can foster a sense of community and social support, which are crucial for emotional well-being."

Which choice best describes the relationship between physical activity and mental health as presented in the passage?

A) Physical activity solely improves cognitive function.
B) Physical activity has multiple benefits, including reducing anxiety and fostering community.
C) Regular exercise is the only way to improve mental health.
D) Social support is more important than physical activity for mental health.

27

"In her groundbreaking work on genetics, Dr. Rosalind Franklin used X-ray crystallography to capture images of DNA that were crucial to understanding its double-helix structure. Although her contributions were initially overlooked, her research laid the foundation for the Nobel Prize-winning discoveries of Watson and Crick."

Which choice best captures the central idea of the passage?

A) Dr. Rosalind Franklin used X-ray crystallography in her research.
B) The double-helix structure of DNA was discovered by Watson and Crick.
C) Dr. Rosalind Franklin's research was crucial to understanding DNA's structure, despite being initially overlooked.
D) Nobel Prize-winning discoveries often rely on foundational research.

Reading and Writing test – Module 2
32 Minutes, 27 Questions
Direction

The questions in this section address a number of important reading and writing skills. Each question includes one or more passages, which may include a table or graph. Read each passage and question carefully, and then choose the best answer to the question based on the passage(s). All questions in this section are multiple-choice with four answer choices. Each question has a single best answer.

1

The writer Olivia Green is celebrated for her minimalist storytelling. Her ability to _____ complex emotions into brief narratives has garnered critical acclaim.

Which choice completes the text with the most logical and precise word or phrase?

A) simplify
B) condense
C) elaborate
D) obscure

2

The following text is from a classic adventure novel.

The protagonist recounts his decision to embark on a solo journey across the desert. He describes the vast, unpredictable landscape and the sense of freedom that drew him to this adventure.

Which choice best describes the function of the underlined sentence in the text as a whole?

A) It sets the stage for the protagonist's journey.
B) It introduces the main conflict of the novel.
C) It provides a detailed description of the desert.
D) It explains why the protagonist dislikes city life.

3

In 2018, urban planner Laura Green conducted a study on the impact of city parks on community well-being. She found that access to green spaces significantly _____ residents' mental health and life satisfaction.

Which choice completes the text with the most logical and precise word or phrase?

A) worsened
B) enhanced
C) neglected
D) hindered

4

The following text is from a fantasy novel by a contemporary author.

The hero embarks on a quest to retrieve a magical artifact. Along the way, he encounters various mythical creatures and overcomes numerous obstacles.

Which choice best describes the function of the underlined sentence in the text as a whole?
A) It sets up the main plot of the novel.
B) It introduces a secondary character.
C) It describes the setting of the story.
D) It explains the hero's motivations.

5

In 2017, Dr. Sarah Thompson researched the effects of plastic pollution on marine life. Her findings revealed that ingestion of plastic particles _____ the health of various ocean species.

Which choice completes the text with the most logical and precise word or phrase?

    A) enhanced
    B) ignored
    C) compromised
    D) improved

6

The painter Vincent van Gogh is famous for his vibrant, emotive paintings. His use of bold colors and dynamic brushstrokes _____ the intensity of his emotional experiences.

Which choice completes the text with the most logical and precise word or phrase

    A) obscures
    B) diminishes
    C) conveys
    D) contradicts

7

In 2021, Dr. Ava Brown conducted a study on the impact of meditation on stress reduction. She found that regular meditation practice significantly _____ stress levels and improved overall well-being.

Which choice completes the text with the most logical and precise word or phrase?

    A) increased
    B) confused
    C) elevated
    D) reduced

8

The following text is from a science fiction novel by a modern author.

Captain Lee leads her crew on a mission to explore a newly discovered planet. They encounter alien life forms and must navigate complex political tensions between different species.

Which choice best describes the function of the underlined sentence in the text as a whole?

    A) It sets up the main plot of the novel.
    B) It introduces a secondary character.

C) It describes the setting of the story.

D) It explains the protagonist's background.

9

The following passage is from a scientific journal article on quantum entanglement:

"Recent experiments have demonstrated that quantum entanglement, once thought to be limited to subatomic particles, can be observed in macroscopic objects. This breakthrough challenges our understanding of quantum mechanics and its relationship to classical physics, potentially bridging the gap between these two seemingly disparate realms."

Which of the following best captures the main implication of this passage?

A) Quantum entanglement is no longer a valid scientific concept.

B) Classical physics and quantum mechanics are completely unrelated fields.

C) The boundary between quantum and classical physics may be less distinct than previously thought.

D) Macroscopic objects behave exactly like subatomic particles in all circumstances.

10

In her landmark work on social psychology, Dr. Amelia Chen posits that human behavior is shaped by a complex interplay of genetic predispositions, environmental factors, and individual choices. This nuanced view challenges both genetic determinism and the "blank slate" theory of human nature.

Which of the following statements best represents Dr. Chen's perspective on human behavior?

A) Genetic factors are the sole determinants of human behavior.

B) Environmental influences completely override genetic predispositions.

C) Individual choices are made independently of genetic and environmental factors.

D) Human behavior results from a dynamic interaction of multiple influences.

11

In 2016, environmental scientist Dr. Samuel White conducted a study on the impact of climate change on coastal ecosystems. His findings suggest that rising sea levels _____ coastal habitats, threatening biodiversity.

Which choice completes the text with the most logical and precise word or phrase?

A) stabilize

B) erode

C) ignore

D) enhance

12

The following text is from a historical novel set in the 1800s.

Claire, a young woman, reflects on her journey from a small village to the bustling city. She contemplates the changes she has experienced and the new opportunities that lie ahead.

Which choice best describes the function of the underlined sentence in the text as a whole?

A) It introduces the main character.
B) It sets up the central theme of the novel.
C) It describes the setting of the story.
D) It explains the plot of the novel.

13

In 2020, sociologist Dr. Emily Harris studied the effects of social media on adolescents. She found that excessive use of social media can lead to feelings of isolation and anxiety, highlighting the _____ impact of technology on mental health.

Which choice completes the text with the most logical and precise word or phrase?

A) beneficial
B) ambiguous
C) adverse
D) minimal

14

The author Gabriel García Márquez is renowned for his use of magical realism. His novel "One Hundred Years of Solitude" _____ the boundaries between reality and fantasy, creating a unique narrative style.

Which choice completes the text with the most logical and precise word or phrase?

A) blurs
B) defines
C) eliminates
D) restricts

15

The following text is from a contemporary fantasy novel.

Lena embarks on a quest to find an ancient artifact that is said to grant immense power. Along her journey, she faces numerous challenges and uncovers hidden truths about her past.

Which choice best describes the function of the underlined sentence in the text as a whole?
A) It introduces a new character.

B) It provides background information about Lena.

C) It summarizes the main plot of the novel.

D) It describes the setting of the story.

16

In 2018, environmental activist Daniel Green led a campaign to ban single-use plastics in his city. His efforts resulted in a significant _____ in plastic waste and increased public awareness about environmental issues.

Which choice completes the text with the most logical and precise word or phrase?

A) increase

B) decline

C) stabilization

D) neglect

17

The following text is from a critical analysis of modern architecture:

"The Bauhaus movement, with its emphasis on form following function, revolutionized 20th-century design. However, critics argue that this utilitarian approach often resulted in sterile, impersonal spaces that prioritized efficiency over human comfort and aesthetic pleasure."

Which choice best describes the function of the underlined sentence in the text as a whole?

A) It introduces a counterargument to the praised aspects of the Bauhaus movement.

B) It explains why the Bauhaus movement was universally accepted.

C) It provides historical context for the development of modern architecture.

D) It suggests that efficiency and aesthetic pleasure are always mutually exclusive in design.

18

The following text is from a psychological thriller novel.

Detective Morgan uncovers a series of clues that lead her to suspect a prominent businessman of a string of crimes. As she delves deeper into the case, she faces increasing danger and moral dilemmas.

Which choice best describes the function of the underlined sentence in the text as a whole?

A) It introduces the main character.

B) It sets up the central conflict of the novel.

C) It describes the setting of the story.

D) It explains the detective's motivations.

19

Recent paleoclimatological studies have revealed that Earth's climate has undergone rapid shifts in the past, sometimes within the span of a few decades. This discovery has led some scientists to _____ the possibility of abrupt climate change in our current era, emphasizing the need for proactive measures to mitigate potential risks.

Which choice completes the text with the most logical and precise word or phrase?

    A) dismiss
    B) reevaluate
    C) overlook
    D) exaggerate

20

The philosopher Immanuel Kant proposed that space and time are not objective features of the world, but rather _____ structures imposed by the human mind to organize sensory experience. This revolutionary idea, known as transcendental idealism, challenged prevailing notions of reality and perception.

Which choice completes the text with the most logical and precise word or phrase?

    A) arbitrary
    B) subjective
    C) physical
    D) irrelevant

21

The following text is from a classic American novel.

The protagonist reflects on his journey across the country, encountering a diverse array of people and experiences. His travels lead him to a deeper understanding of himself and the world around him.

Which choice best describes the function of the underlined sentence in the text as a whole?

    A) It introduces the main character.
    B) It summarizes the central theme of the novel.
    C) It describes the setting of the story.
    D) It explains the purpose of the protagonist's journey.

22

Scholars often cite Charles Dickens' experiences growing up in poverty as a major influence on his writing, but many do not recognize his work as reflecting broader social critiques. In fact, Dickens authored numerous novels and essays addressing various societal issues. Thus, those who primarily view Dickens' work as autobiographical _____

Which choice most logically completes the text?

A) overlook the many other factors that motivated Dickens to write.
B) risk misrepresenting the full range of Dickens' contributions to literature.
C) may draw inaccurate conclusions about how Dickens viewed his own experiences.
D) tend to interpret Dickens' work in an overly personal context.

23

Lila walked through the dense forest, the canopy of leaves above casting dappled shadows on the path. She paused to listen to the distant sound of a flowing stream, feeling a sense of peace and solitude.

The scene primarily emphasizes Lila's experience of _____.

    A) navigating a challenging terrain
    B) finding tranquility in nature
    C) searching for a lost item
    D) encountering wildlife

24

In the bustling café, patrons chatted loudly while baristas prepared coffee drinks with practiced efficiency. Sophie found a quiet corner and pulled out her laptop, ready to focus on her writing despite the surrounding noise.

Sophie's main challenge in this scene is to _____.

    A) find a seat in the crowded café
    B) enjoy the lively atmosphere
    C) concentrate on her writing amid the noise
    D) get the baristas' attention

25

The old barn stood at the edge of the field, its wooden walls weathered and faded by years of exposure to the elements. Tom examined the barn with interest, noting its historical significance and the potential for restoration.

Tom's interest in the barn is primarily due to its _____.

    A) potential for agricultural use
    B) historical value and restoration opportunities
    C) current condition and maintenance needs
    D) proximity to his home

26

During the community meeting, residents voiced their concerns about the new development project. The debate was lively, with differing opinions on how the project would impact local traffic and housing.

The focus of the community meeting is on _____.

A) improving local infrastructure
B) addressing concerns about the development project
C) planning a neighborhood event
D) electing new community leaders

27

The young musician played a hauntingly beautiful melody on her violin, captivating the audience with her expressive performance. The room fell silent as listeners were absorbed in the music.

The impact of the musician's performance on the audience is best described as _____.

A) distracting
B) moving
C) confusing
D) unimpressive

Math test – Module 1
35 Minutes, 22 Questions
Directions

The questions in this section address a number of important math skills.

Use of a calculator is permitted for all questions.

NOTES

- Unless otherwise indicated:
- All variables and expressions represent real numbers.
- Figures provided are drawn to scale.
- All figures lie in a plane.
- The domain of a given function f is the set of all real numbers x for which

is a real number.

Reference

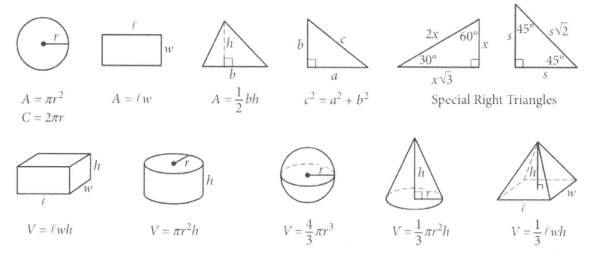

$A = \pi r^2$ $A = \ell w$ $A = \frac{1}{2} bh$ $c^2 = a^2 + b^2$ Special Right Triangles

$C = 2\pi r$

$V = \ell wh$ $V = \pi r^2 h$ $V = \frac{4}{3} \pi r^3$ $V = \frac{1}{3} \pi r^2 h$ $V = \frac{1}{3} \ell wh$

Source: https://yocket.com/us/wp-content/uploads/2024/02/SAT-math-forumla.png

- 360 degrees is the number of arc degrees in a circle.

- A circle has two radians of arc, or 2p.

- A triangle's total angle measurements, expressed in degrees, equals 180.

For multiple-choice questions, solve each problem, select the correct answer from the options provided, and then circle your answer in this book. Only circle one answer per question. If you change your mind, completely erase the previous circle. You will not receive credit for questions with more than one answer circled or for questions with no answer circled.

For student-produced response questions, solve each problem and write your answer next to or under the question in the test book as follows:

- Do not include symbols such as a percent sign, comma, or dollar sign in your circled answer.
- Once you've written your answer, circle it clearly. You will not receive credit for anything written outside the circle or for any questions with more than one circled answer.
- If you find more than one correct answer, write and circle only one.
- Your answer can be up to 5 characters for a positive answer and up to 6 characters (including the negative sign) for a negative answer.
- If your answer is a fraction that exceeds the character limit (over 5 characters for positive, 6 characters for negative), write the decimal equivalent.
- If your answer is a decimal that exceeds the character limit (over 5 characters for positive, 6 characters for negative), truncate or round it to the fourth digit.
- If your answer is a mixed number (such as 3½), write it as an improper fraction (7/2) or its decimal equivalent (3.5).

1. 2x-y=8

x+2y=4

What is the value of x + y in the above system of equations?

    A) –1
    B) 4
    C) 5
    D) 20

2. What can be substituted for $2(x^2 - x) + 3(x^2 - x)$ in this equation?

    A) $5x^2 - 5x$
    B) $5x^2 - 5x$
    C) $5x^2$
    D) 5x

3. Regarding the graph of the equation 2x – 3y = –4 in the xy-plane, which of the following propositions is true?

    A) The y-intercept is positive and the slope is negative.
    B) Both the slope and the y-intercept are negative.
    C) Both the slope and the y-intercept are positive.
    D) The y-intercept is negative and the slope is positive.

4. A roller coaster car's front is located 15 feet above the ground at the base of a hill. Which of the following equations provides the height h, in feet, of the roller coaster car's front seconds after it starts up the ride if the front rises at a constant rate of 8 feet per second?

    A) h = 8s + 15
    B) h = 15s + 335/8
    C) h =8s + 335/15

D) h = 15s + 8

5. C= 75h + 125

The given calculation provides the value of C in US dollars. An electrician bills by the hour for labor-intensive tasks. This electrician was employed by both Mr. Roland and Ms. Sanchez. Compared to Mr. Roland's job, the electrician spent two hours more working for Ms. Sanchez. How much more did Ms. Sanchez pay the electrician than did Mr. Roland?

    A) $75
    B) $125
    C) $150
    D) $275

6.

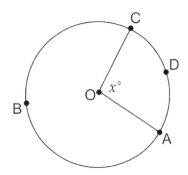

The center of the circle above is O, arc length (ADC) = 5π, and x = 100. What is the arc ABC's length?

    A) 9.00
    B) 13.11.
    C) 18.11.
    D) 25.13

7. What is the value of x if 8/x = 160?

    A) 1,280
    B) 80
    C) 20
    D) 0.05

8. 2ax-15=3(x+3)+5(x-1)

The constant an in the given equation. If the value of What is the value of a when x fulfills the equation?

    A) 1
    B) 2
    C) 4
    D) 8

9.

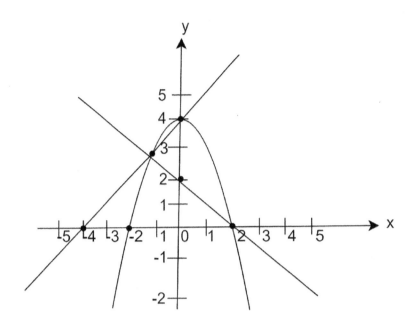

The above xy plane graphs a system of three equations. How many different ways may the system be solved?

 A) Nothing
 B) One
 C) Two
 D) Three

10. $(ax - 3)(5x^2 - bx + 4) = 20x^3 - 9x^2 - 2x + 12$

For all x, where a and b are constants, the equation above holds true. What does ab stand for?

 A) 18
 B) 20
 C) 24
 D) 40

11. $\frac{x}{x-3} = \frac{2x}{3}$

Which of the following sums up all the values of x that can possibly meet the given equation?

 A) Zero and Two
 B) Zero and Four
 C) -4 and Four
 D) Four

12. $\frac{1}{2x+1} + 5$ For x > 0, which of the following expressions is equivalent?

A) . $\frac{2x+5}{2x+1}$

B) . $\frac{2x+6}{2x+1}$

C) . $\frac{10x+5}{2x+1}$

D) . $\frac{10x+6}{2x+1}$

13.

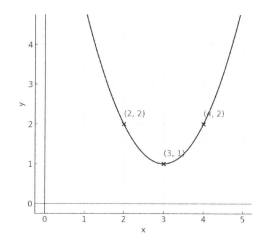

A parabola is the graph of the function f in the above xy plane. Which definition of f applies to this? The following examples show how to calculate fx:

A) $f(x) = 4(x - 3)^2 + 1$
B) $f(x) = 4(x + 3)^2 + 1$
C) $f(x) = (x - 3)^2 + 1$
D) $f(x) = 3(x + 3)^2 + 1$

$$y \geq x+2$$

$$2x + 3y \leq 6$$

14. Which of the following best describes the solution set in the xy-plane to the above system of inequalities that the gray region represents?

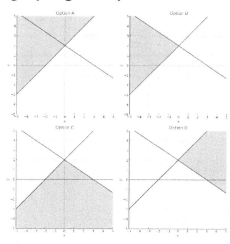

15. What is the set of all the solutions to the equation $\sqrt{x+2}$=-x?

A) {−1, 2}
B) {−1}
C) {2}
D) There are no solutions to the given equation.

16. What has to be true for all values of x if sin x° = a?

A) $\cos x° = a$
B) $\sin 90° - ° = (\ ) \times a$
C) $\cos (90° - x°) = a$
D) $\sin (x2)° = a$

17. h(x)=-16x+100x+10 A projectile thrown vertically and at a height of h feet above the ground x seconds later is represented by the quadratic function above. What does the positive x-intercept of a graph representing y h = (x) mean in the actual world if the graph is drawn in the xy-plane?

A) The projectile's starting height
B) The projectile's highest possible point
C) The instant the bullet reaches its highest point in the sky
D) The instant the missile touches down

18. What is the volume of a right rectangular prism with a length of 4 cm, measured in cubic centimeters?

19. 4x + 2 = 4 If x is such that the following equation holds, what is the value of 2x +1?

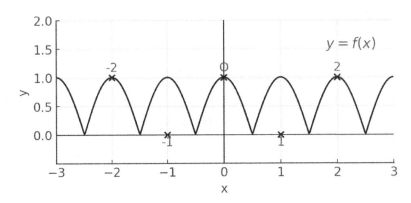

20. The entire graph of the function f on the xy plane is displayed in the above figure. The formula g(x) f(x) = + 6 defines the function g (not displayed). What is the function g's maximum value?

21. Right angle Q exists in triangle PQR. In the event that Sin R = 4/5, what is the tan P value?

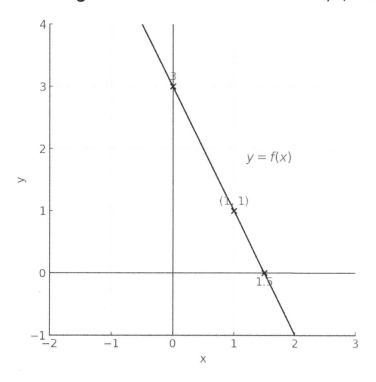

22. In the xy plane above, the linear function f's graph is displayed. The linear function g's graph, which is not displayed, is perpendicular to the f's graph and passes through the points (1, 3). How much does g(0) mean?

Math test – Module 2
35 Minutes, 22 Questions
Directions

The questions in this section address a number of important math skills.

Use of a calculator is permitted for all questions.

NOTES

- Unless otherwise indicated:
- All variables and expressions represent real numbers.
- Figures provided are drawn to scale.
- All figures lie in a plane.
- The domain of a given function f is the set of all real numbers x for which

is a real number.

Reference

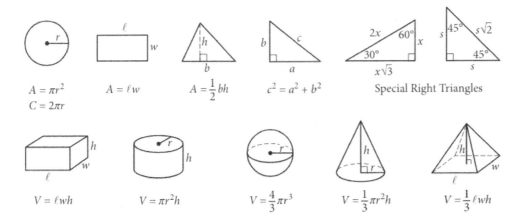

$A = \pi r^2$ $A = \ell w$ $A = \frac{1}{2} bh$ $c^2 = a^2 + b^2$ Special Right Triangles
$C = 2\pi r$

$V = \ell wh$ $V = \pi r^2 h$ $V = \frac{4}{3}\pi r^3$ $V = \frac{1}{3}\pi r^2 h$ $V = \frac{1}{3}\ell wh$

Source: https://yocket.com/us/wp-content/uploads/2024/02/SAT-math-forumla.png

- 360 degrees is the number of arc degrees in a circle.
- A circle has two radians of arc, or 2p.
- A triangle's total angle measurements, expressed in degrees, equals 180.

For multiple-choice questions, solve each problem, select the correct answer from the options provided, and then circle your answer in this book. Only circle one answer per question. If you change your mind, completely erase the previous circle. You will not receive credit for questions with more than one answer circled or for questions with no answer circled.

For student-produced response questions, solve each problem and write your answer next to or under the question in the test book as follows:

- Do not include symbols such as a percent sign, comma, or dollar sign in your circled answer.
- Once you've written your answer, circle it clearly. You will not receive credit for anything written outside the circle or for any questions with more than one circled answer.
- If you find more than one correct answer, write and circle only one.
- Your answer can be up to 5 characters for a positive answer and up to 6 characters (including the negative sign) for a negative answer.
- If your answer is a fraction that exceeds the character limit (over 5 characters for positive, 6 characters for negative), write the decimal equivalent.
- If your answer is a decimal that exceeds the character limit (over 5 characters for positive, 6 characters for negative), truncate or round it to the fourth digit.
- If your answer is a mixed number (such as 3½), write it as an improper fraction (7/2) or its decimal equivalent (3.5).

1. Which number of x makes the formula 3 + 3 = 27 x true?

(A) 3
B) 8
C) 10

D) 27

2. In ancient Egypt, there were two measures of length used: cubits and palms. One cubit is equal to seven palms. About 140 cubits is the length of the Great Sphinx statue in Giza. Which of the subsequent best describes the Great Sphinx statue's length, measured in palms?

A) 0.05
B) 20
C) 140
D) 980

3. In the event when 2n/5 = 10, what is the value of 2n −1?

A) 24
B) 49
C) 50
D) 99

4. $\sqrt{x^2} = x$ Of the following, which value of x is NOT a solution to the above equation?

A) -4%
B) 0%
C) 1
D) 3%

The following details are referred to in questions 5 and 6.

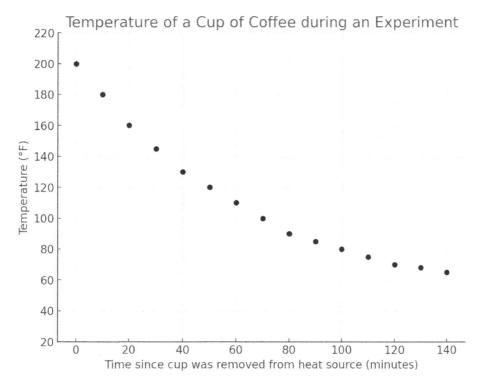

Temperature of a Cup of Coffee during an Experiment

A heated cup of coffee is taken out of a heat source and placed in a temperature-controlled environment for the purpose of this experiment. The above graph displays the coffee's temperature in degrees Fahrenheit (°F) both immediately after it is taken off of the heat source and then every ten minutes after that.

5. Which of the following accurately describes the temperature of the coffee when it is first taken out of the heat source, in degrees Fahrenheit?

    A) 75
    B) 100
    C) 155
    D) 195

6. In which of the subsequent ten-minute intervals does the coffee's temperature drop the fastest on average?

    A) From 0 to 10 minutes;
    B) From 30 to 40 minutes;
    C) From 50 to 60 minutes;
    D) From 90 to 100 minutes

7.

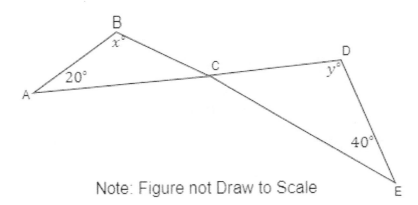

Note: Figure not Draw to Scale

AD and BE cross at C in the aforementioned figure. What is the value of y if x = 100?

    A) 100
    B) 90
    C) 80
    D) 60

8. The line graphed in the xy-plane below represents the entire cost of a taxi ride in a certain city, denoted by y, in dollars.

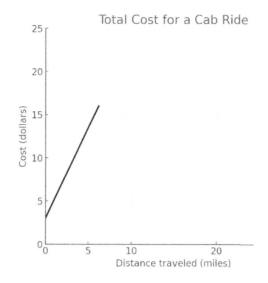

Total Cost for a Cab Ride

According to the number of miles traveled, x, during off-peak hours. What is the price per unit based on the graph?

A) $2.00;
B) $2.60;
C) $3.00;
D) $5.00

9.

Customer Purchases at a Gas Station

	Beverage purchased	Beverage not purchased	Total
Gasoline purchased	60	25	85
Gasoline not purchased	35	15	50
Total	95	40	135

A nearby petrol station saw 135 patrons on Tuesday. The aforementioned table presents a summary of the fuel purchases made by consumers on Tuesday. drink, neither, or both. How likely is it, given the information in the table, that a random gas station customer that day did not buy gasoline?

A) 15/50
B) 15/40
C) 35/50
D) 50/135

10. Washington High School freshmen, sophomores, juniors, and seniors were chosen at random.

for a survey regarding possible schedule adjustments for the next year. Four of the students that were chosen for the survey were freshmen, and three were sophomores. Juniors made up half of the remaining chosen students. How many of the 336 students who were chosen to participate in the survey were seniors?

    A) 240
    B) 140
    C) 120
    D) 70

11. At the moment, Plant B is 12 centimeters tall, and Plant A is 20 centimeters tall. The height ratio of Plant C to Plant D is the same as the height ratio of Plant A to Plant B. What is the height of Plant D, measured in centimeters, if Plant C is 54 cm tall?

    A) 32.4
    B) 44.0
    C) 62.0
    D) 90.0

12. At the Beebe Vent Field, the deepest underwater vent in the world, scientists discovered a new species of pale shrimp. 3.1 miles below the surface of the sea is the vent.

How many kilometers does the vent extend below the surface of the sea? (1 mile = 0.6214 kilometers)

    A), 2
    B), 3
    C), 4
    D), 5

13. Only shipments weighing 100 pounds or 120 pounds are delivered by a freight helicopter. The helicopter may only transport a maximum of 1,100 pounds worth of items on each delivery flight, and it must carry at least 10 packages overall. How many packages weighing 120 pounds can the helicopter hold on a single trip?

    A) 2,
    B), 4
    C), 5
    D) 6

14. A $120,000 equipment was acquired by a corporation. The machine's worth decreases by the same amount an annual sum, so that in ten years the value will be $30,000. Which of the following formulas provides the machine's value, v, in dollars, t years after it was bought for $0 \leq 10 \leq t$?

    A) v = 30,000 − 9,000t
    B) v = 120, 000 − 9, 000t
    C) v = 120,000 + 9,000t
    D) v = 120,000 − 30,000t

15. The points (2, 4) and (0, 1) are on line m in the xy-plane. Which of the following describes a line m equation?

    A) y = 2x +3
    B) y = 2x +4
    C) y = 3/2x + 3
    D) y= 3/2x + 1

16. $(4x + 4)(ax − 1) − x^2 + 4$ In the expression above, a is a constant. If the expression is equivalent to bx, where b is a constant, what is the value of b ?

    A) −5
    B) −3
    C) 0
    D) 12

17. If 2w + 4t = 14 and 4w + 5t = 25 , what is the value of 2w +3t ?

    A) 6
    B) 10
    C) 13
    D) 17

Information below is mentioned in questions 18–20.

Cereal Crunchy Grain was purchased by Jennifer. The nutritional information on the package indicates that a serving size of the Cereal contains 210 calories in a quarter-cup serving, of which 50 come from fat. Moreover, 180 mg of potassium, or 5% of the adult daily need, are provided by each cereal meal.

18. If eating x servings of Crunchy Grains cereal a day provides an adult with p percent of their daily potassium allowance, which of the following best describes p in terms of x?

    A) p = 0.5x;
    B) p = 5x;
    C) p = 0.05 (x);
    D) p = 1.05 x in each case.

19. Jennifer's plan for her Tuesday breakfast is to combine Crunchy Grain and Super Grain cereal. Fantastic Cereal made of grains has 240 calories per cup. How many calories (270) does a cup of Jennifer's mixture contain if it contains that much Super Grain cereal?

A) 1/8 cup
B) 1½ cups
C) 3¼ cups
D) A half-cup

20. Which of the following might represent the graph showing the amount of fat-based calories in Crunchy Grain cereal based on the quantity of 3 four cups worth of cereal?

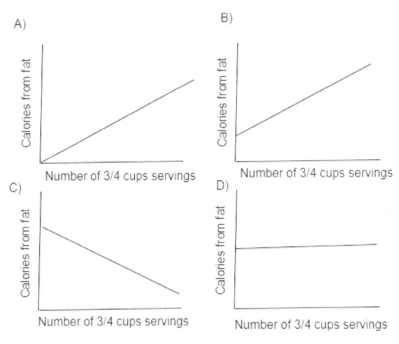

21. With y h = (x), the exponential function h's graph in the xy-plane has a y-intercept of d. where a positive constant, d, is used. Which of the subsequent could be used to define the function h?

A) H(x) = −3 d
B) h(x) = 3(x) d
C) h(x) = d(− x) 3
D) h (x)= d(3)

22. The weights of fifteen horses in a stable were recorded in pounds, and the data's mean, median, range, and standard deviation were discovered. It was discovered that the horse that had the lowest recorded weight actually weighed 10 pounds less than that. If the four values are reported using the corrected weight, which value stays the same?

A) Median;
B) Range;
C) Mean
D) Standard Deviation

PRACTICE TEST #2

Reading and Writing test - Module 1
32 Minutes, 27 Questions
Direction

The questions in this section address a number of important reading and writing skills. Each question includes one or more passages, which may include a table or graph. Read each passage and question carefully, and then choose the best answer to the question based on the passage(s). All questions in this section are multiple-choice with four answer choices. Each question has a single best answer.

1

Social animals such as primates, birds, and humans display an innate attraction to faces. Dr. Sofia Ramos and her team tested whether this trait occurs in solitary reptiles, specifically desert tortoises. Using an image of three dots arranged like eyes and a mouth, they found that hatchlings showed a preference for the face-like pattern, suggesting that _____

Which choice most logically completes the text?

A) face-like stimuli are likely perceived as harmless by solitary species without parental care.

B) researchers should not assume that an innate attraction to faces is related to social behavior.

C) the attraction to face-like stimuli is likely innate rather than learned.

D) newly hatched tortoises show a stronger preference for face-like stimuli than adults do.

2

Compiled in the early 1600s through the efforts of local historians, "The Chronicles of Kyoto" is a significant collection of Japanese historical accounts. The texts describe life in Kyoto before the city's modernization, and annotations in the Chronicles indicate that much of the content predates major foreign influences. Nonetheless, some entries contain references to foreign customs and technologies. Thus, some historians have concluded that _____

Which choice most logically completes the text?

A) while its content largely predates modernization, "The Chronicles of Kyoto" also contains later additions.

B) although those who compiled "The Chronicles of Kyoto" were fluent in Japanese, they had limited knowledge of foreign languages.

C) before foreign influences, Japanese historians borrowed from other cultures' literary traditions.

D) the references to foreign customs should be attributed to coincidental resemblances.

3

In a study of the problem-solving abilities of raccoons, researchers failed to account for the physical difficulty of the tasks. Raccoons given simple tasks like lifting a lid were evaluated using the same criteria as those given complex tasks like opening a latch. The results of the study, therefore, _____

Which choice most logically completes the text?

A) could suggest differences in cognitive ability among the raccoons that may not actually exist.

B) are useful for identifying tasks raccoons can perform but not for evaluating their cognitive limits.

C) should not be taken as indicative of the problem-solving abilities of any species other than raccoons.

D) reveal more about the raccoons' physical dexterity than their cognitive abilities.

4

To survive during periods of drought, the embryos of certain amphibians enter a state of suspended animation known as diapause. In this state, development pauses, allowing the embryos to remain viable for extended periods.

Which choice completes the text so that it conforms to the conventions of Standard English?

A) enter

B) to enter

C) having entered

D) entering

5

The intense pressure in the deep ocean can distort proteins in the cells of marine organisms. The compound trimethylamine N-oxide (TMAO) helps proteins maintain their shape under such conditions and is found in high concentrations in the cells of deep-sea fish.

Which choice completes the text so that it conforms to the conventions of Standard English?

A) configurations. TMAO

B) configurations TMAO

C) configurations, TMAO

D) configurations and TMAO

6

Food and the sensation of taste play a significant role in the works of novelist Monique Truong. In "The Book of Salt," for example, the character of Bình connects to his homeland through the food he prepares, while in "Bitter in the Mouth," the character of Linda _____ a form of synesthesia where words evoke tastes.

Which choice completes the text so that it conforms to the conventions of Standard English?

    A) experienced
    B) had experienced
    C) experiences
    D) will be experiencing

7

Inventor Sam Taylor created a prototype of the first flexible straw by inserting a screw into a plastic tube and using thread to bind the tube tightly around the screw. When the thread and screw were removed, the resulting ridges allowed the straw to bend easily.

Which choice completes the text so that it conforms to the conventions of Standard English?

    A) screw's thread's.
    B) screws' threads.
    C) screw's threads.
    D) screws threads'.

8

Golden orb-weaver spiders are brightly colored and do not appear to use camouflage to capture their prey. These spiders wait conspicuously in the center of their webs for insects to approach. Researcher Dr. Lisa Kim of the University of Melbourne has suggested that the spider's distinctive coloration might actually attract prey.
Which choice completes the text so that it conforms to the conventions of Standard English?

    A) prey, rather,
    B) prey rather,
    C) prey, rather;
    D) prey; rather,

9

In Death Valley's Racetrack Playa, 162 rocks of varying sizes move periodically, leaving trails in the sediment that mark their mysterious migration.

Which choice completes the text so that it conforms to the conventions of Standard English?

A) playas sediment mark the rock's
B) playa's sediment mark the rocks
C) playa's sediment mark the rocks'
D) playas' sediment mark the rocks'

10

In her fantasy novels, Nigerian-British author Helen Oyeyemi often draws inspiration from classic fairy tales. Her novel "Boy, Snow, Bird" is a retelling of Snow White, while her novel "Gingerbread" offers a twist on the tale of Hansel and Gretel.

Which choice completes the text so that it conforms to the conventions of Standard English?

A) Gingerbread—
B) Gingerbread,
C) Gingerbread
D) Gingerbread:

11

The novel's plot is _____, with unexpected twists that keep readers engaged until the very end.

Which choice completes the text with the most logical and precise word or phrase?

A) predictable
B) convoluted
C) suspenseful
D) straightforward

12

The committee's recommendation to _____ the old building was met with both praise and criticism from the community.

Which choice completes the text with the most logical and precise word or phrase?

A) preserve
B) demolish
C) renovate
D) ignore

13

The teacher emphasized the importance of _____ in academic writing, encouraging students to develop their own voice and style.

Which choice completes the text with the most logical and precise word or phrase?

A) clarity
B) imitation
C) uniformity

D) complexity

14

While researching a topic, a student has taken the following notes:

- Mount Everest is the highest peak in the world at 29,032 feet.
- K2 is the second-highest peak at 28,251 feet.
- Both mountains are part of the Himalayan range.
- The first successful ascent of Everest was in 1953 by Sir Edmund Hillary and Tenzing Norgay.
- K2 was first successfully climbed in 1954 by an Italian team.

The student wants to highlight the significance of these mountains. Which choice most effectively uses relevant information from the notes to accomplish this goal?

A) Mount Everest and K2 are the two highest peaks in the world, with Everest being climbed first in 1953.
B) The Himalayan range includes Mount Everest and K2, the highest and second-highest peaks in the world.
C) Both Mount Everest and K2 were first successfully climbed in the 1950s.
D) Sir Edmund Hillary and Tenzing Norgay were the first to climb Everest, while an Italian team first climbed K2.

15

The marketing campaign was highly effective, resulting in a significant _____ in sales.

Which choice completes the text with the most logical and precise word or phrase?

A) decrease
B) fluctuation
C) increase
D) stability

16

The city council's decision to _____ the park was met with widespread approval from residents.

Which choice completes the text with the most logical and precise word or phrase?

A) neglect
B) expand
C) privatize
D) abandon

17

The book provides a comprehensive overview of the topic, making it an _____ resource for students and professionals alike.

Which choice completes the text with the most logical and precise word or phrase?

A) invaluable
B) outdated
C) irrelevant
D) obscure

18

Jamie stood in the crowded subway station, watching the people rush past her. She glanced at her watch and realized she was running late for her meeting. The loud announcements and the bustling crowd made it hard to concentrate.

In this scene, Jamie's primary concern is _____.

A) finding a quieter place
B) getting to her meeting on time
C) enjoying the subway ride
D) observing the crowd

19

As the sun set over the small town, the streets grew quiet. The only sound was the occasional bark of a distant dog. Sarah sat on her porch, sipping tea and reflecting on the day's events.

The atmosphere described in the scene is best characterized as _____.

A) chaotic
B) tranquil
C) noisy
D) hectic

20

Alex flipped through the pages of the old journal he found in the attic. Each entry was filled with elaborate drawings and handwritten notes about adventures and dreams long past.

The journal's entries are primarily described as _____.

A) mundane and practical
B) colorful and imaginative
C) factual and detailed
D) short and fragmented

21

The kitchen was filled with the aroma of freshly baked bread. Emma carefully placed the loaves on the cooling rack and admired the golden-brown crusts, feeling a sense of accomplishment.

The primary focus of the scene is on _____.

    A) the process of baking bread
    B) Emma's feeling of satisfaction
    C) the kitchen's aroma
    D) the appearance of the bread

22

At the annual fair, children ran from one booth to another, their laughter mingling with the sounds of carnival games. The bright lights and colorful tents created an atmosphere of excitement.

The mood of the fair is best described as _____.

    A) somber
    B) festive
    C) tense
    D) subdued

23

Rachel opened the letter and scanned the handwritten lines. The words were heartfelt and filled with apologies, but Rachel could not shake the feeling of disappointment.

Rachel's reaction to the letter is one of _____.

    A) surprise
    B) contentment
    C) frustration
    D) indifference

24

In the library's quiet reading room, John found a secluded corner where he could focus on his research. The soft hum of the air conditioning was the only sound breaking the silence.

The setting of the reading room is best described as _____.

    A) noisy and bustling
    B) calm and focused
    C) crowded and lively
    D) chaotic and distracting

25

The artist's studio was filled with canvases covered in bright, abstract patterns. Paintings of various sizes and colors lined the walls, each one telling a different story.

The description of the studio emphasizes _____.

A) the artist's use of color
B) the artist's organizational skills
C) the studio's cleanliness
D) the artist's preference for realism

26

As the storm raged outside, Mark sat by the fireplace, reading a book. The crackling fire and the rhythmic patter of rain against the window created a cozy and safe retreat.

The atmosphere inside Mark's house is best characterized as _____.

A) cold and uninviting
B) warm and comforting
C) damp and uncomfortable
D) noisy and distracting

27

The town's historical society held an exhibition featuring artifacts from the early 1900s. Visitors marveled at the antique items and learned about the town's rich history.

The purpose of the exhibition is to _____.

A) sell historical artifacts
B) entertain visitors with modern displays
C) educate the public about the town's history
D) promote new historical research

Reading and Writing test - Module 2
32 Minutes, 27 Questions
Direction

The questions in this section address a number of important reading and writing skills. Each question includes one or more passages, which may include a table or graph. Read each passage and question carefully, and then choose the best answer to the question based on the passage(s). All questions in this section are multiple-choice with four answer choices. Each question has a single best answer.

1

In 1995, the novel "Shadows in the Forest" was co-written by Maria Sanchez and David Lee, standing out as a prime example of _____ in the literary world. Despite their successful collaboration, the experience strained their friendship, highlighting why many authors prefer to work solo.

Which choice completes the text with the most logical and precise word or phrase?

A) experimentation
B) innovation
C) cooperation
D) competition

2

The current methods of mechanically recycling plastics are often deemed _____ due to their environmental impact and the degradation of material quality that often ensues. However, chemist Sarah Taylor has pioneered a cleaner process of chemical recycling that transforms superabsorbent polymers from diapers into a valuable reusable adhesive.

Which choice completes the text with the most logical and precise word or phrase?

A) efficient
B) inadequate
C) complicated
D) traditional

3

Interruptions in the supply chain for semiconductors used in consumer electronics have challenged an analyst's prediction that sales of these devices will see significant growth in the near future. Although these delays are unlikely to _____ her forecast entirely, they will almost certainly push back the timeline.

Which choice completes the text with the most logical and precise word or phrase?

A) reinforce
B) confirm
C) alter
D) negate

4

For her 2022 art installation, Harmony, artist Lisa Wu collaborated with musician and composer Jordan Rivers to create a piece that critics deemed truly _____. They praised Wu for ingeniously converting a gallery space into a vibrant exhibit, projecting images of Rivers onto a large canvas and filling the room with the sound of his and other voices singing.

Which choice completes the text with the most logical and precise word or phrase?

A) captivating
B) traditional

C) confusing
D) monotonous

5

The organization's outreach program was designed to _____ the community and provide essential services to those in need.

Which choice completes the text with the most logical and precise word or phrase?

A) isolate
B) divide
C) empower
D) exploit

6

Despite facing numerous challenges, the team managed to _____ the project ahead of schedule.

Which choice completes the text with the most logical and precise word or phrase?

A) abandon
B) delay
C) complete
D) sabotage

7

The new restaurant quickly gained popularity due to its _____ menu and excellent customer service.

Which choice completes the text with the most logical and precise word or phrase?

A) limited
B) diverse
C) overpriced
D) bland

8

Text 1: Some economists argue that technological unemployment—job loss due to technological change—is a temporary phenomenon. They contend that while technology may eliminate certain jobs, it also creates new opportunities and industries, ultimately leading to a net positive effect on employment.

Text 2: Recent studies on the impact of artificial intelligence and automation suggest that the rate of job displacement may outpace job creation in the coming decades. This trend could lead to widespread unemployment and increasing income inequality if not addressed through policy interventions and education reform.

How does Text 2 relate to the argument presented in Text 1?

A) It provides supporting evidence for the economists' view in Text 1.
B) It offers an alternative perspective that challenges the optimistic view in Text 1.
C) It elaborates on the specific industries mentioned in Text 1.
D) It proposes a compromise between conflicting views on technological unemployment.

9

The following text is adapted from Hannah Green's 1935 poem "Urban Nights in Spring."

Night wears a garment
All velvet soft, all violet blue...
And over her face she draws a veil
As shimmering fine as floating dew...
And here and there
In the black of her hair
The subtle hands of Night
Move slowly with their gem-starred light.

Which choice best describes the overall structure of the text?

A) It contrasts descriptions of night in different settings.
B) It transitions from a depiction of night to dawn.
C) It uses an extended metaphor comparing night to a person.
D) It describes how night varies across seasons.

10

According to historian Laura Martinez, Latina women played pivotal roles in the labor movement during the 1940s. During this time, manufacturing companies signed contracts to supply the United States military with essential goods. The increased production demands gave workers, many of whom were Latina women, greater bargaining power: they demanded better benefits, and employers, eager to meet contract deadlines, complied. Thus, labor activism became a platform for Latina women to assert their influence.

Which choice best describes the function of the underlined portion in the text as a whole?

A) It expands on a point about labor relations in a specific industry mentioned earlier.
B) It provides an example of an economic trend during the World War II era.
C) It identifies a potential outlier in the labor activism narrative presented earlier.
D) It offers more information about the workers discussed previously.

11

The following text is adapted from the short story "The Journey Home" by Sarah Williams, published in 1925. Ten-year-old Emma lived in a small village surrounded by dense woods. Her vivid imagination and love for daydreaming puzzled the village folk. A small river

JUPITER DIGITAL EXAM PREP

flowed just beyond her backyard, its banks lined with willows, oaks, and birches. The water was dotted with colorful lily pads. Emma loved to wander to the water's edge, toss in small twigs, and watch them drift downstream, dreaming of the distant lands they might reach and wishing she could follow them.

Which choice best describes the function of the underlined sentence in the text as a whole?

    A) It elaborates on the scenery of a place Emma enjoys visiting.
    B) It indicates that some villagers are perplexed by Emma's actions.
    C) It highlights the distinctiveness of Emma's imagination.
    D) It implies that Emma yearns for a life beyond her village.

12

The following text is adapted from Oscar Wilde's 1891 novel "The Picture of Dorian Gray." Dorian Gray is taking his first look at a portrait that Hallward has painted of him.

Dorian passed listlessly in front of his picture and turned towards it. When he saw it he drew back, and his cheeks flushed for a moment with pleasure. A look of joy came into his eyes, as if he had recognized himself for the first time. He stood there motionless and in wonder, dimly conscious that Hallward was speaking to him, but not catching the meaning of his words. The sense of his own beauty came on him like a revelation. He had never felt it before.

According to the text, what is true about Dorian?

    A) He wishes to hear Hallward's thoughts on the portrait.
    B) He is captivated by his own likeness in the painting.
    C) He favors portraits over other art forms.
    D) He doubts Hallward's artistic abilities.

13

The novel "Whispering Pines" by Emma Roberts, published in 2005, is a rare example of _____ in contemporary literature. Roberts co-authored the book with her longtime friend, yet the process strained their relationship, underscoring why many authors prefer to write solo.

Which choice completes the text with the most logical and precise word or phrase?

    A) competition
    B) partnership
    C) imitation
    D) individualism

14

The traditional method of recycling aluminum cans is often seen as _____ due to the energy-intensive processes and environmental impact involved. However, engineer Paul

Stevens has developed a new approach that significantly reduces energy consumption and improves efficiency.

Which choice completes the text with the most logical and precise word or phrase?

A) sustainable
B) outdated
C) revolutionary
D) practical

15

Supply chain disruptions for raw materials in the automotive industry have put into question the assertion that the sector will see substantial growth this year. These interruptions are unlikely to _____ the forecast completely, but they will definitely prolong the expected recovery period.

Which choice completes the text with the most logical and precise word or phrase?

A) confirm
B) enhance
C) invalidate
D) support

16

For her 2023 sculpture series Reflections, artist Maya Johnson collaborated with architect Daniel Park to create works that critics found truly _____. They commended Johnson for transforming public spaces with interactive installations that engaged viewers on multiple levels.

Which choice completes the text with the most logical and precise word or phrase?

A) conventional
B) predictable
C) innovative
D) ordinary

17

Some biologists have argued that reptiles in the Triassic period were not a particularly _____ group. However, Dr. Elena Ramirez's research suggests that these ancient reptiles displayed a remarkable variety of forms and behaviors. Fossils found in Argentina reveal species with unique adaptations, such as Gliding Lizardus, which Dr. Ramirez believes could glide between trees.

Which choice completes the text with the most logical and precise word or phrase?

A) diverse
B) singular
C) typical
D) mundane

18

The novel "Silent Echoes," published in 2010 by Lisa Carter, is celebrated for its _____ use of language, which draws readers into the story's rich and atmospheric setting.

Which choice completes the text with the most logical and precise word or phrase?

A) monotonous
B) vivid
C) technical
D) obscure

19

The entrepreneur's innovative approach to business has not only increased profits but also _____.

Which choice completes the text with the most logical and precise word or phrase?

A) reduce employee satisfaction
B) improved community relations
C) complicated the supply chain
D) undermined brand reputation

20

When they were first introduced to Western Europe from Byzantium in the eleventh century, table forks were met with much resistance. The Bishop of Ostia, St. Peter Damian, condemned the eating utensils because he considered _____ dangerous and unnecessary luxury items.

Which choice completes the text so that it conforms to the conventions of Standard English?

A) them
B) this
C) that
D) it

21

The council voted to implement the new policy immediately, despite concerns from some members about its potential _____.

Which choice completes the text with the most logical and precise word or phrase?

A) benefits
B) outcomes
C) advantages
D) drawbacks

22

The artist's latest exhibition, which features a series of sculptures made from recycled materials, _____ the importance of sustainability in modern art.

Which choice completes the text with the most logical and precise word or phrase?

A) illustrates
B) complicates
C) neglects
D) diminishes

23

The company's decision to expand internationally was driven by a desire to _____.

Which choice completes the text with the most logical and precise word or phrase?

A) increase market share
B) reduce operational costs
C) streamline domestic operations
D) limit product offerings

24

The politician's speech was characterized by _____ statements and emotional appeals, aiming to rally support from the public.

Which choice completes the text with the most logical and precise word or phrase?

A) ambiguous
B) vague
C) emphatic
D) factual

25

The main advantage of the new software is its ability to _____.

Which choice completes the text with the most logical and precise word or phrase?

A) increase productivity
B) confuse users
C) limit functionality
D) raise costs

26

Despite initial skepticism, the scientist's findings were eventually _____ by the broader scientific community.

Which choice completes the text with the most logical and precise word or phrase?

A) ignored
B) rejected
C) embraced
D) questioned

27

The researcher's innovative method has the potential to _____ the field of biotechnology.

Which choice completes the text with the most logical and precise word or phrase?

A) revolutionize
B) complicate
C) undermine
D) standardize

Math test – Module 1
35 Minutes, 22 Questions
Directions

The questions in this section address a number of important math skills.

Use of a calculator is permitted for all questions.

NOTES

Unless otherwise indicated:

- All variables and expressions represent real numbers.
- Figures provided are drawn to scale.
- All figures lie in a plane.
- The domain of a given function f is the set of all real numbers x for which

is a real number.

Reference

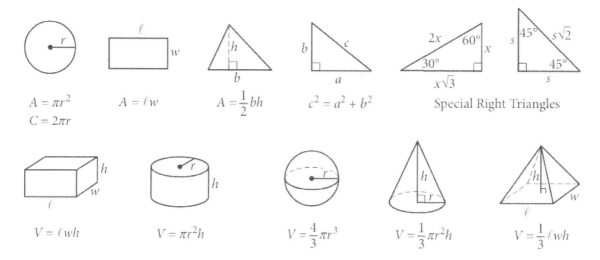

$A = \pi r^2$ $A = \ell w$ $A = \frac{1}{2}bh$ $c^2 = a^2 + b^2$ Special Right Triangles
$C = 2\pi r$

$V = \ell wh$ $V = \pi r^2 h$ $V = \frac{4}{3}\pi r^3$ $V = \frac{1}{3}\pi r^2 h$ $V = \frac{1}{3}\ell wh$

Source: https://yocket.com/us/wp-content/uploads/2024/02/SAT-math-forumla.png

- 360 degrees is the number of arc degrees in a circle.
- A circle has two radians of arc, or 2p.
- A triangle's total angle measurements, expressed in degrees, equals 180.

For multiple-choice questions, solve each problem, select the correct answer from the options provided, and then circle your answer in this book. Only circle one answer per question. If you change your mind, completely erase the previous circle. You will not receive credit for questions with more than one answer circled or for questions with no answer circled.

For student-produced response questions, solve each problem and write your answer next to or under the question in the test book as follows:

- Do not include symbols such as a percent sign, comma, or dollar sign in your circled answer.
- Once you've written your answer, circle it clearly. You will not receive credit for anything written outside the circle or for any questions with more than one circled answer.
- If you find more than one correct answer, write and circle only one.
- Your answer can be up to 5 characters for a positive answer and up to 6 characters (including the negative sign) for a negative answer.
- If your answer is a fraction that exceeds the character limit (over 5 characters for positive, 6 characters for negative), write the decimal equivalent.
- If your answer is a decimal that exceeds the character limit (over 5 characters for positive, 6 characters for negative), truncate or round it to the fourth digit.
- If your answer is a mixed number (such as 3½), write it as an improper fraction (7/2) or its decimal equivalent (3.5).

1. Salam wishes to buy tennis match tickets from a dealer. The supplier levies a one-time service charge for handling the ticket purchases. To find the total amount T in dollars that Salim will pay for n tickets, use the equation T n = 15 + 12. What in the equation does 12 stand for?

A) One ticket's cost, expressed in US dollars
B) The service charge total, expressed in US dollars
C) The entire cost of one ticket, in dollars, that Salim will pay
D) The total sum that Salim is willing to pay in USD for whatever number of tickets

2. A landscaper purchases two types of fertilizer. 60% of the weight of fertilizer A is made up of filler components, and By weight, 40% of fertilizer B is made up of filler components.

The gardener purchased fertilizers that together comprise 240 pounds of filler material.

Where x is the number of pounds of fertilizer A and y is the number of pounds of fertilizer B, which equation best represents this relationship?

A) 0.4x + 0.6y = 240
B) 0.6x + 0.4y = 240
C) 40x + 60y = 240
D) 60x + 40y = 240

3. Given two complex numbers, 2+3i and 4+8i, where i = -1 what is the total of them?

A) 17
B) 17i
C) 6 + 11i
D) 8 + 24i

4. $4x^2 - 9 = (px + t)(px = t)$

P and t in the above equation are constants.

What may the value of p be, out of the following?
A) 2
B) 3
C) 4
D) 9

5. Which of the following describes the xy-plane graph of the equation y = 2 −5 x?

A)
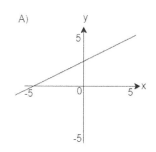

B)
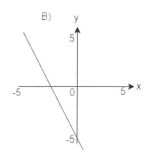

C)
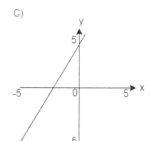

D)
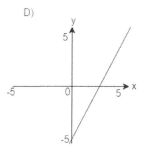

6. When x = 2/3 y and When y = 18, what does 2x −3 mean?

A)21
B) 15
C) 12
D) 10

7. A bricklayer can calculate the number of bricks, n, required to construct a wall that is A feet long and h feet high using the formula n = 7lh. Which of the following describes A in terms of n and h correctly?

A) $l = \dfrac{7}{nh}$

B) $l = \dfrac{h}{7n}$

C) $l = \dfrac{n}{7h}$

D) $l = \dfrac{n}{7+h}$

8.

x	w	t (x)
1	-1	-3
2	3	-1
3	4	1
4	3	3
5	-1	5

The table above shows some values of the functions w and t. For which value of x is w(x)+ t(x) = x ?

A) 1
B) 2
C) 3
D) 4

9. If $\sqrt{x} + \sqrt{9} = \sqrt{64}$, what is the value of x ?

A) $\sqrt{5}$
B) 5
C) 25
D) 55

10. Jaime is training for a cycling competition. His objective is to ride his bike at least 280 kilometers a week on average for 4 weeks. In the first, second, and third weeks, he rode his bike 240 miles, 310 miles, and 320 miles. Which inequality may be used to show how many miles, x, Jaime would need to ride his bicycle in the fourth week in order to reach his goal?

A) 240 + 310 + 320/3 + ≥ 280
B) 240 + 310 + 320 ≥ x(280)
C) 240/4 + 310/4 + 320/4 + x≥ 280
D) 240 + 310 + 320 + x≥ 4 (280)

11.

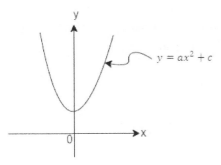

In the xy plane above, the parabola's vertex is (0,c). Regarding the parabola with the equation $y = -c(x - b)^2 + c$ which of the following statements is true?

A) The graph widens upward, and the vertex is (b c).
B) The graph opens downward, and the vertex is (b c).
C) The graph widens upward, and the vertex is (−b c).

D) The graph opens downward and the vertex is (−b c).

12. Of the following, which one equals $\frac{4x^2+6x}{4x+2}$?

A) x

B) x + 4

C) $x - \frac{2}{4x+2}$

D) $x + 1 - \frac{2}{4x+2}$

13. $2x^2 - 4x = t$ **Here, t is a constant in the given equation. Which of the following might be the value of t if there are no true solutions to the equation?**

A) - 3

B) - 1

C) 1

D) 3

14. Laundry services purchase fabric softener and detergent from their provider. The vendor will produce in a package, no more than 300 pounds. The weight of each detergent bottle is 7.35 pounds, while the weight of each fabric softener container is 6.2 pounds. The service requests to purchase a minimum of twice as many detergent containers as fabric softener containers. For each set of numbers d and s, which are nonnegative integers, stand for the number of detergent and fabric softener containers, respectively. Which of the following inequality systems most accurately describes this circumstance?

A) 7.35d + 6.2s ≤ 300
   D ≥ 2s

B) 7.35d + 6.2s ≤ 300
   d ≥ 2s

C) 14.7d + 6.2s ≤ 300
   D ≥ 2s

D) 14.7d + 6.2s ≤ 300
   2d ≥s

15. Which of the following is equivalent to $(a + \frac{b}{2})^2$?

A) $a^2 + \frac{b^2}{2}$

B) $a^2 + \frac{b^2}{4}$

C) $a^2 + \frac{ab}{2} + \frac{b^2}{2}$

D) $a^2 + ab + \frac{b^2}{4}$

16.

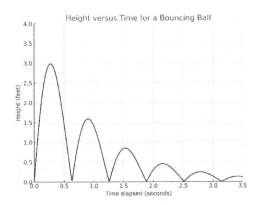

A ball was dropped as part of an experiment, and it was allowed to bounce off the ground several times before coming to rest. The chart above illustrates this correlation between the ball's height above the ground and the amount of time that passed after it was dropped. How many times was the ball at least two feet high after it was dropped?

A) One;
B) Two;
C) Three;
D) Four

17. The monthly water bill for one customer was $75.74. Her monthly price has increased to $79.86 as a result of a rate rise. How much did the customer's water bill increase by, to the nearest tenth of a percent?

A) 4.1%;

B) 5.1%;

C) 5.2%;

D) 5.4% 25

18. When a_4^b = 16 Given two positive integers, a and b, what is the maximum value that b might have?

19. 2/3 t= 5/2 What is the answer to the preceding equation for the value of t?

20.

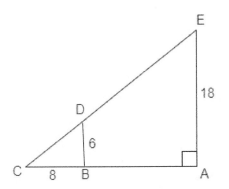

BD and AE are parallel in the given figure. What is the duration of the CE?

21. To get three liters of a 10% saline solution, how many liters of a 25% saline solution must be added 15% solution of salt?

22. Arc pAB has a length of π 3 and points A and B are located on a circle with radius 1. What percentage of the circle's circumference is the length of arc pAB?

Math test – Module 2
35 Minutes, 22 Questions
Directions

The questions in this section address a number of important math skills.

Use of a calculator is permitted for all questions.

NOTES

Unless otherwise indicated:

- All variables and expressions represent real numbers.
- Figures provided are drawn to scale.
- All figures lie in a plane.
- The domain of a given function f is the set of all real numbers x for which

is a real number.

Reference

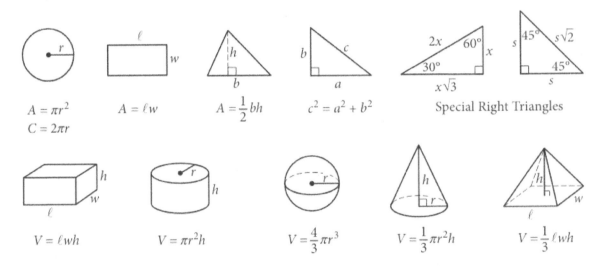

$A = \pi r^2$ $A = \ell w$ $A = \frac{1}{2} bh$ $c^2 = a^2 + b^2$ Special Right Triangles

$C = 2\pi r$

$V = \ell wh$ $V = \pi r^2 h$ $V = \frac{4}{3}\pi r^3$ $V = \frac{1}{3}\pi r^2 h$ $V = \frac{1}{3}\ell wh$

Source: https://yocket.com/us/wp-content/uploads/2024/02/SAT-math-forumla.png

- 360 degrees is the number of arc degrees in a circle.
- A circle has two radians of arc, or 2p.
- A triangle's total angle measurements, expressed in degrees, equals 180.

For multiple-choice questions, solve each problem, select the correct answer from the options provided, and then circle your answer in this book. Only circle one answer per question. If you change your mind, completely erase the previous circle. You will not receive credit for questions with more than one answer circled or for questions with no answer circled.

For student-produced response questions, solve each problem and write your answer next to or under the question in the test book as follows:

- Do not include symbols such as a percent sign, comma, or dollar sign in your circled answer.
- Once you've written your answer, circle it clearly. You will not receive credit for anything written outside the circle or for any questions with more than one circled answer.
- If you find more than one correct answer, write and circle only one.
- Your answer can be up to 5 characters for a positive answer and up to 6 characters (including the negative sign) for a negative answer.
- If your answer is a fraction that exceeds the character limit (over 5 characters for positive, 6 characters for negative), write the decimal equivalent.
- If your answer is a decimal that exceeds the character limit (over 5 characters for positive, 6 characters for negative), truncate or round it to the fourth digit.
- If your answer is a mixed number (such as 3½), write it as an improper fraction (7/2) or its decimal equivalent (3.5).

1. That expression $(2x^2 - 4)(-3x^2 + 2x - 7)$ is equivalent to which?

A) $5x^2 - 2x + 3$
B) $5x^2 + 2x - 3$
C) $-x^2 - 2x - 11$
D) $-x^2 + 2x - 11$

2.

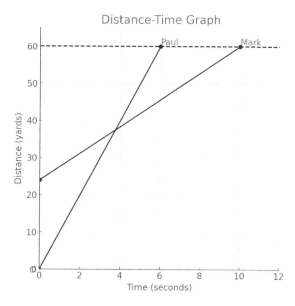

The graph above shows the positions of Paul and Mark during a race. Paul and Mark each ran at a constant rate, and Mark was given a head start to shorten the distance he needed to run. Paul finished the race in 6 seconds, and Mark finished the race in 10 seconds. According to the graph, Mark was given a head start of how many yards?

A) 3
B) 12
C) 18

D) 24

3. The snow ceased for a while after falling. The snow fell back again, but this time it did so more quickly than it had at first. Which of the following graphs best represents the total amount of snow accumulation over time, assuming that none of the snow melted during the specified period?

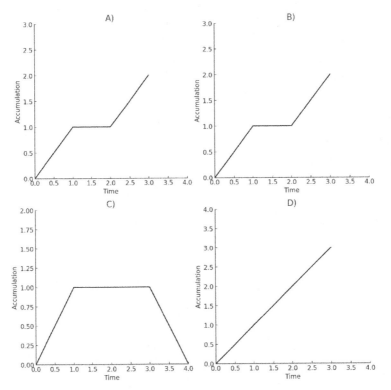

4. Businesses that use website hosting services pay a one-time setup fee of $350 + dollars for each

month. What is the worth of d if a business owner paid $1,010 for the first 12 months, including the startup fee?

A) 25
B) 35
C) 45
D) 55

5. 6x-9y>12

Which of the subsequent inequality types is the same as the inequality mentioned above?

A) x-y>2
B) 2x −3y >4
C) 3x −2y >4
D) 3x −2y >2

6.

Where Do People Get Most of Their Medical Information?

Source	Percent of those
Doctor	63%
Internet	13%
Magazines/brochures	9%
Pharmacy	6%
Television	2%
Other/none of the	7%

A summary of 1,200 survey responses is displayed in the table above. How many of persons questioned, according to the table, receive the majority of their medical data from the Internet or a physician?

A) 865;
B) 887;
C) 912;
D) 926

7. The goal of the city council was to determine what the views of all citizens were on the conversion of a field that is open to a dog park. A sample of 500 dog owners in the city was polled by the council. The majority of individuals surveyed, according to the study, supported the dog park. About the survey conducted by the city council, which of the following is true?

A) It demonstrates that most city dwellers support the dog park.
B) A larger proportion of locals who own dogs ought to have been included in the survey sample.
C) Only locals without dogs should have been included in the survey sample.
D) Because the survey sample is not typical of all city dwellers, it is skewed.

8.

		Flavor	
		Vanilla	Chocolate
Topping	Hot fudge	8	6
	Caramel	5	6

The ice cream flavors and toppings selected by partygoers are displayed in the above table.

Everybody choose a single ice cream flavor and just one garnish. What percentage of those who selected vanilla ice cream also selected hot fudge as a topping?

A) 8/25
B) 5/13
C) 13/25
D) 8/13

9. A coastal city has a total area of 92.1 square miles, of which 11.3 square miles are made up of water. Should the city possess a with a population of 621,000 in 2010, which of the following best describes the city's population density at that time, measured in persons per square mile of land area?

   A) 6,740
   B) 7,690
   C) 55,000
   D) 76,000

10. Between 1497 and 1500, Amerigo Vespucci embarked on two voyages to the New World. According to Vespucci's letters, the first voyage lasted 43 days longer than the second voyage, and the two voyages combined lasted a total of 1,003 days. How many days did the second voyage last?

   A) 460
   B) 480
   C) 520
   D) 540

11. $7x+3y =8$

$6x -3y =5$

For the solution (x,y) to the system of equations above, what is the value of x-y ?

   A) -4/3
   B) 2/3
   C) 4/3
   D) 22/3

Questions 12 through 14 refer to the data below.

	Day	Height (cm)
0	0.0	0.0
1	7.0	17.93
2	14.0	36.36
3	21.0	67.76
4	28.0	98.1
5	35.0	131.0
6	42.0	169.5
7	49.0	205.5
8	56.0	228.3
9	63.0	247.1
10	70.0	250.5
11	77.0	253.8
12	84.0	254.5

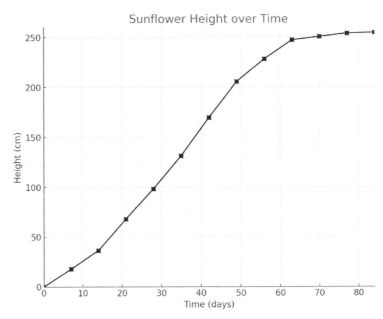

A paper about sunflower growth was published in 1919 by H. S. Reed and R. H. Holland. A sunflower's height, h, measured in centimeters, is displayed in the table and graph above, which are part of the publication following the emergence of the sunflower.

12. What is the sunflower's lowest average growth rate throughout the following periods of time?

A) Day 0 to Day 21;
B) Day 21 to Day 42;
C) Day 42 to Day 63;
D) Day 63 to Day 84.

13. The table below shows the height of a sunflower over a period of days. Based on the information provided, what is the approximate rate of growth in centimeters per day from day 14 to day 35?

Day	Height (cm)
14	36.36
35	131.00

A) 3.5 cm/day
B) 4.5 cm/day
C) 5.5 cm/day
D) 6.5 cm/day

14. A sunflower's growth rate is almost steady from day 14 to day 35. Between now and now, which of the which of the following formulas most accurately describes the sunflower's height h, measured in centimeters, t days after it starts to grow?

A) $h = 2.1t - 15$
B) $h = 4.5t - 27$
C) $h = 6.8t - 12$
D) $h = 13.2t - 18$

15.

x	1	2	3	4	5
y	$\frac{11}{4}$	$\frac{25}{4}$	$\frac{39}{4}$	$\frac{53}{4}$	$\frac{67}{4}$

Which of the following equations, for the values in the preceding table, connects y to x?

A) $y = 1/2 \cdot \left(\frac{5}{2}\right)^{x}$
B) $y = 2 \cdot \left(\frac{3}{4}\right)^{x}$
C) $y = 3/4x + 2$
D) $y = 7/2x - 3/4$

16.

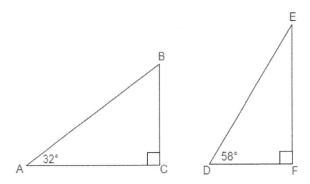

Above are triangles ABC and DEF. Which of the subsequent sums up to the ratio BC AB?

A) DE/DF
B) DF/EF
C) DF/EF
D) EF/DE

Questions 17 through 19 make reference to the data below.

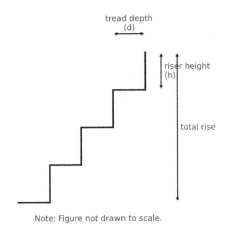

Note: Figure not drawn to scale.

An architect can utilize the riser-tread formula 2 + = 25 h d, where h is the riser height in inches and d is the tread depth in inches, when building a staircase. Every stairway has the same tread depths and riser heights for every step. A stairway's riser count equals the number of steps in the staircase. For instance, the stairs in the accompanying illustration has five steps. As seen in the image, the overall climb of a stairway is equal to the sum of the riser heights.

17. Which of the following expresses the riser height in terms of the tread depth?

A) h= 1/2 (25 +d)
B) h = 1/2 (25 -d)

C) h = -1/2 (25 +d)
D) h = -1/2 (25 -d)

18. According to certain construction requirements, the tread depth of indoor staircases must be at least 9 inches. and a minimum of 5 inches must be the riser height. Which of the following inequalities, based on the riser-tread formula, best captures the set of all potential riser height

values that satisfy this code requirement?

A) h ≥ 5 h
B) 0 ≤ ≤5 h
C) 5 ≤ ≤8 h
D) 8 ≤ ≈ 16 h 19

19. An architect wishes to create a staircase with an odd number of steps, a riser height of between 7 and 8 inches, and a total climb of 9 feet using the riser-tread formula. Which of the following must be the stairway's tread depth, measured in inches, given the architect's constraints?

A) 7.2
B) 9.5
C) 10.6
D) 15

20. What is the total of the answers to (x-6)(x+0.7)=0 ?

A) −6.7
B) −5.3
C) 5.3
D) 6.7

21. A study was conducted on the weights of various fish species in a pond. To make sure that no fish were weighed more than once, a random sample of fish were captured and marked. Out of the 150 largemouth bass in the sample, 30% weighed more than two pounds. Which of the following conclusions does the sample data best support?

A) Most of the fish in the pond are under two pounds in weight.
B) The fish in the pond weigh around two pounds apiece on average.
C) Of all the fish in the pond, about 30% weigh more than two pounds.
D) Of all the largemouth bass in the pond, about 30% weigh more than two pounds.

22.

Number of States with 10 or More Electoral Votes in 2008

Electoral votes	Frequency
10	4
11	4
12	1
13	1

15	3
17	1
20	1
21	2
27	1
31	1
34	1
55	1

The chart above indicates that 21 states received 10 or more electoral votes in 2008. How many electoral votes was the median, according to the table votes in favor of the 21 states?

A) 13
B) 15
C) 17
D) 20

★ ★ ★ ★ ★

SUBMIT A REVIEW

Did these pages help, inspire, or bring you value in any way? If so, we'd love to hear your thoughts through an honest review on Amazon. Your feedback is incredibly valuable to us!

It's very simple and only takes a few minutes:

1. Go to the "My Orders" page on Amazon and search the book.
2. Select "Write a product review".
3. Select a Star Rating.
4. Optionally, add text, photos, or videos and select Submit.

CHAPTER 12
SOLUTIONS AND EXPLANATIONS

PRACTICE TEST 1 ANSWERS

Reading and Writing test - Module 1

Question 1
Option B is the right one. The poet Maya Angelou is known for her powerful and evocative verses. Her poetry often explores themes of identity, resilience, and the human experience.

Question 2
Option A is the right one. The following text is from Ralph Ellison's 1952 novel "Invisible Man." The protagonist navigates a society that refuses to see him, struggling with issues of identity and invisibility. This underlined sentence introduces a major theme of the novel.

Question 3
Option C is the right one. In 2017, historian Dr. Laura Green published a book on the cultural impact of the Renaissance. She argued that the period's emphasis on humanism and individualism shaped modern Western thought.

Question 4
Option A is the right one. The scientist Nikola Tesla is best known for his contributions to the development of alternating current (AC) electricity. His innovative ideas and inventions transformed the field of electrical engineering.

Question 5
Option B is the right one. The following text is from Leo Tolstoy's 1877 novel "Anna Karenina." Anna reflects on her life choices and the consequences of her actions. Her internal struggle reveals the complexities of her emotions and desires. This underlined sentence provides insight into Anna's character development.

Question 6
Option B is the right one. In 2016, Dr. Sam Parker conducted a study on the effects of urbanization on bird populations. He discovered that some bird species have adapted their nesting habits to thrive in city environments.

Question 7
Option C is the right one. The author J.K. Rowling is known for her Harry Potter series, which has captured the imaginations of readers worldwide with its magical world and compelling characters.

Question 8
Option A is the right one. The following text is from Ernest Hemingway's 1952 novella "The Old Man and the Sea." Santiago, an old fisherman, battles a giant marlin far out in the Gulf Stream. The struggle between the man and the fish highlights themes of perseverance and dignity. This underlined sentence introduces the main conflict of the story.

Question 9

Option A is the right one. In 2020, Dr. Lisa Wong conducted a study on the benefits of early childhood education. Her research indicated that children who attend preschool programs experience better academic and social outcomes later in life.

Question 10

Option B is the right one. The musician Miles Davis is celebrated for his contributions to jazz music. His innovative approach and willingness to redefine traditional boundaries have left a lasting impact on the genre.

Question 11

Option B is the right one. As the first Indigenous leader of the modern era, Chief Nako became one of the most prominent figures in his nation's history: during his leadership (2000–2015), Chief Nako strengthened the central government and advocated for environmental preservation.

Question 12

Option A is the right one. Due to their often abstract themes, unconventional syntax, and complex imagery, many of Emma Brown's poems can be quite challenging to understand and thus are the subject of much debate among literary critics.

Question 13

Option C is the right one. The sudden appearance and rapid diversification of animal life in the fossil record about 540 million years ago is referred to as the Cambrian explosion. Some scientists suggest that this abrupt change could be due to the development of hard body parts that are more likely to fossilize.

Question 14

Option B is the right one. During a 2015 archaeological excavation in Greece, researchers uncovered the remains of a woman buried with valuable artifacts from the Early Bronze Age. This discovery might lead scholars, who have long believed Bronze Age societies were male-dominated, to accept that women may have also held significant power.

Question 15

Option D is the right one. In some species of deep-sea fish, individuals develop an additional swim bladder—a seemingly unnecessary formation. Given its prevalence among fish that dive to great depths, some researchers hypothesize that its role isn't random; rather, the additional swim bladder may support diving adaptations.

Question 16

According to an economist, state taxes are secondary to other factors when considering an interstate move. Even significant differences in state taxation have minimal effect on most people's decisions, while differences in job opportunities, housing availability, and climate are strong influences.

Question 17

Option B is the right one. The author's theory about the relationship between Neanderthals and modern humans is flawed because it does not consider recent archaeological discoveries. To be convincing, the argument must address new findings such as the latest Denisovan specimens and Homo longi fossils.

Question 18
Option A is the right one. The following text is from a poem by a contemporary author. Go forth, my child, With dreams that know no bounds! Great adventures, yet unknown, Await Your embrace. I cannot walk with you, My journey is complete, But life is calling you! The main purpose of the text is to encourage a child to embrace the experiences life will offer.

Question 19
Option B is the right one. The following text is adapted from a memoir by a rural farmer. The author describes the traditional methods used by his community to collect honey. The beekeepers began to inspect the hives—moving slowly among them, smoker in hand, and puffing smoke gently to calm the bees. The hives, like people, have their unique traits; some were quick to yield their honey, while others were more resistant. Now, wooden frames were carefully removed, and honeycombs were cut and placed into containers. From these combs—initially trickling, then flowing steadily—the golden honey dripped into the jars. This underlined sentence elaborates on an aspect of the hives that the beekeepers evaluate.

Question 20
Option A is the right one. Text 1 Marine biologists have long puzzled over how numerous species of tiny plankton can coexist in the ocean's surface waters while competing for the same resources. According to conventional theories, one species should eventually dominate. So why do so many species persist? Despite various theories, a satisfactory explanation remains elusive. Text 2 Marine biologist Dr. Lila Johnson and her team have linked plankton diversity to their minute size. These organisms, being so small, are spaced relatively far apart in ocean water and experience it as a dense medium. This separation makes it difficult for them to interact and compete directly. Thus, Johnson's team suggests that direct competition among plankton is less frequent than previously assumed. Johnson and her team would likely respond to the "conventional theories" discussed in Text 1 by arguing that the theories are based on a misunderstanding of plankton competition.

Question 21
Option A is the right one. In 2016, Amelia Quon and her team at a space research organization set out to design a drone capable of flying on Titan, one of Saturn's moons. Due to Titan's dense atmosphere, a standard drone designed for Earth would not generate enough lift. For several years, Quon's team tested various designs in a chamber simulating Titan's atmospheric condition. The final design features longer, faster-rotating blades, enabling the drone to fly in Titan's thick air. According to the text, a drone built for Earth would be unable to fly on Titan because Titan's atmosphere is much denser than Earth's.

Question 22
Option C is the right one. In 2020, Dr. Jamie Carter studied the impact of deforestation on tropical bird species. He found that as forests were cleared, bird populations declined significantly.

Question 23

Option B is the right one. The popularity of electric scooters has led to discussions about safety and infrastructure. Hence, "The popularity of electric scooters has led to discussions about safety regulations and infrastructure adaptation" is the correct choice.

Question 24

Option C is the right one. Urban areas emit more artificial light than estimated, affecting animals and the environment. Hence, "Urban areas emit significantly more artificial light than previously estimated, affecting nocturnal animals and contributing to energy wastage and increased greenhouse gas emissions" is the correct choice.

Question 25

Option B is the right one. To explain the impact of digital media on news consumption. Hence, "The advent of digital media has revolutionized the way people consume news, compelling news organizations to enhance their digital presence and leverage social media to engage with audiences" is the correct choice.

Question 26

Option B is the right one. Physical activity has multiple benefits, including reducing anxiety and fostering community. Hence, "Regular exercise has been shown to reduce symptoms of anxiety and depression, improve mood, and foster a sense of community and social support" is the correct choice.

Question 27

Option C is the right one. Dr. Rosalind Franklin's research was crucial to understanding DNA's structure, despite being initially overlooked. Hence, "Dr. Rosalind Franklin's research was crucial to understanding DNA's structure, despite being initially overlooked" is the correct choice.

Reading and Writing test – Module 2

Question 1

Option B is the right one. Olivia Green's minimalist storytelling is known for its ability to distill complex emotions into concise narratives. The word "condense" precisely captures this ability to take intricate feelings and ideas and present them in a brief yet impactful manner. Thus, "Her ability to condense complex emotions into brief narratives has garnered critical acclaim" is the most logical and precise choice.

Question 2

Option A is the right one. The underlined sentence sets the stage for the protagonist's journey by providing context about his decision to embark on the adventure. It establishes the protagonist's motives and the environment, preparing the reader for the unfolding story. Hence, "It sets the stage for the protagonist's journey" accurately describes the function of the sentence.

Question 3

Option B is the right one. Laura Green's study found that access to green spaces significantly enhances residents' mental health and life satisfaction. The word "enhanced" logically and precisely completes the sentence, indicating the positive impact of green spaces on well-being. Therefore, "She found that access to green spaces significantly enhanced residents' mental health and life satisfaction" is the correct choice.

Question 4
Option A is the right one. The underlined sentence sets up the main plot of the novel by introducing the hero's quest to retrieve a magical artifact and the challenges he will face. This establishes the central narrative that drives the story forward. Thus, "It sets up the main plot of the novel" is the most appropriate description of the sentence's function.

Question 5
Option C is the right one. Dr. Sarah Thompson's findings revealed that ingestion of plastic particles compromised the health of various ocean species. The word "compromised" accurately and precisely completes the sentence, indicating the negative impact of plastic pollution on marine life. Therefore, "Her findings revealed that ingestion of plastic particles compromised the health of various ocean species" is the correct choice.

Question 6
Option C is the right one. Vincent van Gogh's use of bold colors and dynamic brushstrokes conveys the intensity of his emotional experiences. The word "conveys" logically and precisely completes the sentence, capturing how his artistic techniques express his emotions. Thus, "His use of bold colors and dynamic brushstrokes conveys the intensity of his emotional experiences" is the most fitting choice.

Question 7
Option D is the right one. Dr. Ava Brown found that regular meditation practice significantly reduced stress levels and improved overall well-being. The word "reduced" logically and precisely completes the sentence, indicating the positive effect of meditation on stress reduction. Hence, "She found that regular meditation practice significantly reduced stress levels and improved overall well-being" is the correct choice.

Question 8
Option A is the right one. The underlined sentence sets up the main plot of the novel by outlining Captain Lee's mission to explore a newly discovered planet and the challenges she and her crew will face. This establishes the central narrative of the story. Thus, "It sets up the main plot of the novel" accurately describes the function of the sentence.

Question 9
Option C is the right one. The passage discusses a breakthrough where quantum entanglement, typically associated with subatomic particles, has been observed in macroscopic objects. This observation challenges the traditional understanding of quantum mechanics and its relationship to classical physics. The key phrase "bridging the gap between these two seemingly disparate realms" suggests that this discovery blurs the line between quantum and classical physics, making option C the best interpretation of the passage's main implication.

Question 10
Option D is the right one. Dr. Chen's perspective, as described in the passage, emphasizes a "complex interplay" of genetic predispositions, environmental factors, and individual

choices in shaping human behavior. This view is described as "nuanced" and challenges both genetic determinism and the "blank slate" theory. Option D best captures this multi-faceted approach to understanding human behavior, reflecting the dynamic interaction of various influences that Dr. Chen proposes.

Question 11

Option B is the right one. Dr. Samuel White's findings suggest that rising sea levels erode coastal habitats, threatening biodiversity. The word "erode" logically and precisely completes the sentence, indicating the detrimental effects of climate change on coastal ecosystems. Therefore, "His findings suggest that rising sea levels erode coastal habitats, threatening biodiversity" is the correct choice.

Question 12

Option B is the right one. The underlined sentence sets up the central theme of the novel by highlighting Claire's journey and the changes she has experienced, which likely ties into broader themes of personal growth and new opportunities. Thus, "It sets up the central theme of the novel" accurately describes the function of the sentence.

Question 13

Option C is the right one. Dr. Emily Harris found that excessive use of social media can lead to feelings of isolation and anxiety, highlighting the adverse impact of technology on mental health. The word "adverse" logically and precisely completes the sentence, indicating the negative effects of social media. Hence, "She found that excessive use of social media can lead to feelings of isolation and anxiety, highlighting the adverse impact of technology on mental health" is the correct choice.

Question 14

Option A is the right one. Gabriel García Márquez's novel "One Hundred Years of Solitude" blurs the boundaries between reality and fantasy, creating a unique narrative style. The word "blurs" logically and precisely completes the sentence, capturing his blending of these elements. Therefore, "His novel 'One Hundred Years of Solitude' blurs the boundaries between reality and fantasy, creating a unique narrative style" is the correct choice.

Question 15

Option C is the right one. The underlined sentence summarizes the main plot of the novel by outlining Lena's quest to find an ancient artifact and the challenges she faces. This provides a clear overview of the story. Thus, "It summarizes the main plot of the novel" accurately describes the function of the sentence.

Question 16

Option B is the right one. Daniel Green's campaign to ban single-use plastics resulted in a significant decline in plastic waste and increased public awareness about environmental issues. The word "decline" logically and precisely completes the sentence, indicating the reduction in plastic waste. Hence, "His efforts resulted in a significant decline in plastic waste and increased public awareness about environmental issues" is the correct choice.

Question 17

Option A is the right one. The first sentence of the passage introduces the Bauhaus movement positively, highlighting its revolutionary impact on 20th-century design. The underlined sentence, starting with "However," presents a contrasting view. It introduces criticism of the movement, arguing that its utilitarian approach often led to impersonal and sterile spaces. This sentence functions as a counterargument to the initially presented positive aspects of the Bauhaus movement, making option A the correct choice.

Question 18

Option B is the right one. The underlined sentence sets up the central conflict of the novel by outlining Detective Morgan's investigation and the increasing danger and moral dilemmas she faces. This establishes the main narrative tension. Thus, "It sets up the central conflict of the novel" accurately describes the function of the sentence.

Question 19

Option B is the right one. The passage discusses new paleoclimatological evidence showing that Earth's climate has undergone rapid shifts in the past. This discovery is presented as leading scientists to reconsider the possibility of abrupt climate change in our current era. The word "reevaluate" best fits this context, as it implies a careful reassessment of previous assumptions based on new evidence. This reevaluation is linked to the emphasis on proactive measures, suggesting a shift in scientific thinking about climate change possibilities.

Question 20

Option B is the right one. Kant's philosophy of transcendental idealism, as described in the passage, proposes that space and time are not objective features of the world but are imposed by the human mind to organize sensory experience. The term "subjective" best captures this idea, as it refers to something existing in the mind rather than the external, objective world. This concept is described as "revolutionary" and challenging to prevailing notions, emphasizing its departure from objective views of reality.

Question 21

Option B is the right one. The underlined sentence summarizes the central theme of the novel by highlighting the protagonist's journey and the deeper understanding he gains. This ties into the broader themes of self-discovery and exploration. Thus, "It summarizes the central theme of the novel" accurately describes the function of the sentence.

Question 22

Option B is the right one. Those who primarily view Charles Dickens' work as autobiographical risk misrepresenting the full range of Dickens' contributions to literature. The word "risk misrepresenting" logically and precisely completes the sentence, indicating that focusing only on the autobiographical aspect can lead to an incomplete understanding of his work. Hence, "Thus, those who primarily view Dickens' work as autobiographical risk misrepresenting the full range of Dickens' contributions to literature" is the correct choice.

Question 23

Option B is the right one. The scene primarily emphasizes Lila's experience of finding tranquility in nature. Hence, "Lila's experience of peace and solitude in the forest" is the correct choice.

Question 24

Option C is the right one. Sophie's main challenge in this scene is to concentrate on her writing amid the noise. Hence, "Sophie's challenge to focus on her writing despite the café's noise" is the correct choice.

Question 25

Option B is the right one. Tom's interest in the barn is primarily due to its historical value and restoration opportunities. Hence, "Tom's interest in the barn's historical value and potential for restoration" is the correct choice.

Question 26

Option B is the right one. The focus of the community meeting is on addressing concerns about the development project. Hence, "The community meeting's focus on concerns about the development project" is the correct choice.

Question 27

Option B is the right one. The impact of the musician's performance on the audience is best described as moving. Hence, "The musician's performance was moving, captivating the audience and causing them to fall silent" is the correct choice.

Math test - Module 1

Question 1

Option B is the right one. The result of multiplying both sides of the system's initial equation by two is $4x - 2y = 16$. $2y - 4x = 16$ is added to the second $5x = 20$ is the result of the system's equation. $x = 4$ is obtained by dividing both sides of $5x = 20$ by 5. $4 + 2y = 4$ is the result of substituting 4 for x in $x + 2y = 4$. $2y = 0$ is obtained by deducting 4 from both sides of $4 + 2y = 4$. $Y = 0$ is obtained by dividing both sides of this equation by 2. In the expression $x + y$, $4 + 0 = 4$ is obtained by substituting 4 for x and 0 for y

Question 2

Option A is the right one. Since the original expression contains the term "$x^2 - x$," like terms can be added: $2(x^2 - x) + 3(x^2 - x) = 5(x^2 - x)$. $5x^2 - 5x$ is the result of distributing the constant term 5.

Question 3

Option D is the right one. The preceding equation can be rewritten in the slope-intercept form $y = mx + b$ to determine the slope and y-intercept, where The line's slope is denoted by m, and the y-intercept is denoted by b. In slope-intercept form, the above equation $2y - 3x = -4$ can be rewritten as $2y = 3x - 4$ by first adding 3x to both sides of the equation.

Subtracting 2 from both sides of the equation yields the equation $y = 3/2\, x - 2$. The graph's slope is represented by the coefficient of x, which is 3/2, and its y-intercept is represented by the constant term, $- 2$. Consequently, the equation $2y - 3x = -4$ exhibits a positive slope on its graph.

Question 4

Option A is the right one. It goes without saying that the roller coaster car's front begins to rise at 15 feet above the ground. This starting altitude of 15 feet can be expressed in an equation by the constant term 15. The front of the roller coaster car rises eight feet every second, or eight seconds. Thus, the height of the roller coaster car's front in feet is given by the equation h = 8s + 15, which is calculated seconds after the vehicle begins to climb the hill.

Question 5

Option C is the right one. Given that the variable h denotes the quantity of the coefficient of h, 75, indicates the electrician's hours worked on the job. fee per hour, expressed in US dollars, following a $125 one-time set price. Given that the electrician spent an additional two hours working on Ms. Sanchez's job than on Mr. Roland's; hence, the extra fee for Work for Ms. Sanchez is $75 × 2 = $150.

Question 6

Option D is the right one.

First, we need to understand what x represents. In a circle, the central angle is twice the inscribed angle that subtends the same arc. So, x = 100° is the inscribed angle, and the central angle for arc ADC is 200°.

We're given that arc length (ADC) = 5π. We know that a full circle is 360°, so we can set up a proportion: 200° / 360° = 5π / (2πr), where r is the radius of the circle

Simplify: 5/9 = 5π / (2πr) r = 9

Now, we need to find the central angle for arc ABC. Since ADC is 200°, ABC must be 160° (as a full circle is 360°).

We can now set up another proportion to find the length of arc ABC: 160° / 360° = x / (2πr), where x is the length of arc ABC

Substitute r = 9: 160 / 360 = x / (18π) x = (160 * 18π) / 360 = 8π ≈ 25.13

The closest answer to 25.13, which is option D.

Question 7

Option D is the right one. 160x = 8 is the result of multiplying both sides of the given equation by x. Splitting 160x = 8 in half on both sides 160 yields the formula x = $\frac{8}{160}$. When $\frac{8}{160}$ is reduced to its most basic form, the result is x = $\frac{1}{20}$; this is equivalent to 0.05 in decimals.

Question 8

The proper choice is C.

The right answer is choice C. To find the value of the constant a in the given equation when xxx fulfills the equation, follow these steps:

Start with the equation: $2ax-15=3(x+3)+5(x-1)$

First, simplify the right side: $2ax-15=3x+9+5x-5$

Combine like terms on the right side: $2ax-15=8x+4$

Next, set the coefficients of x and the constants equal to each other, since the equation must be true for all values of x: $2a=8-15=4$

Solve for a:

$2a=8$

$a = 8/2$

$a=4$

Therefore, the value of a is 4.

The correct answer is C.

Question 9

Option B is the right one. Any ordered pair (x, y) that has a solution for each of the three equations is a solution to the system of three equations. An ordered pair (x, y) must be a point where all three graphs meet, or it must sit on the graph of each equation in the xy-plane. There is just one location where the graphs of the three equations intersect: (−1, 3). As a result, there is only one solution to the equation system.

Question 10

The correct choice is C. The expressions on both sides of the equation will be equal if the equation holds true for all values of x. The left side of the equation's polynomials can be multiplied to get $5ax^3 - abx^2 + 4ax + 15x 2 - 3bx + 12$. The only x^2 term on the right side of the equation is $-9x^2$. Given the equality of the terms on both sides of the equation, we can write $-abx^2 + 15x^2 = -9x^2$ as $(-ab + 15) x^2 = -9x^2$. Consequently, ab = 24 since −ab + 15 = −9.

Question 11

The correct choice is B. The given equation's right-hand side is rewriteable as x. $X = \frac{x}{x-3}$ is the result of multiplying both sides of the equation _x = x (x - 3) by x − 3. $x = x^2 - 3x$ is the result of applying the distributive property of multiplication to the right-hand side of the equation x = x(x − 3). When one subtracts x from each side of the equation, the result is 0 = $x^2 - 4x$. 0 = x(x − 4) is the result of factoring x from both terms of $x^2 - 4x$. The solutions to the equation 0 = x(x − 4) are x = 0 and x − 4 = 0, or x = 4, according to the zero product property. In the provided equation, substituting 0 and 4 for x results in 0 = 0 and 4 = 4, respectively.

Question 12

The right answer is D. By multiplying the numerator and the original expression, one rational expression may be created. The second term's denominator can be expressed as follows: $\frac{1}{2x+1} + \frac{10x+5}{2x+1}$, which is the denominator of the first term. This formula can now be rewritten as and represents the sum of two rational expressions having a common denominator $\frac{1}{2x+1} + \frac{10x+5}{2x+1} = \frac{10x+6}{2x+1}$.

Question 13

The answer is option C. In vertex form, a parabola's equation is f(x) = a(x − h). 2 + k, where an is a constant and the point (h, k) is the parabola's vertex. The graph indicates that the vertex's coordinates are (3, 1), meaning that h = 3 and k = 1. Consequently, f(x) = a(x − 3)^2 + 1 can be represented as an equation that defines f. Replace a value for x with its matching value for y, or f(x), to find a. For instance, the point (4, 2) on the graph of f. Therefore, a must satisfy the formula 2 = a(4 − 3)^2 + 1, which can also be expressed as 1 = a(1)^2 or a = 1. Thus, f(x) is an equation that defines f.

Question 14

Option B is the right one. The first inequality's solutions, y ≥ x + 2, are found on or above the line that passes through y = x + 2. (0, 2) and (−2, 0). By dividing 2x + 3y ≤ 6 by 3 on both sides, which provides 2, and then subtracting 2 from both sides, which yields y ≤ − 2/3 x + 2, the second inequality can be recast in slope intercept form. The line that crosses through (0, 2) and (3, 0) is y = − 2 /3 x + 2, and the solutions to this inequality are on or below it. Choice B is the only graph where the shaded area satisfies these requirements.

Question 15

Option B is the right one. The preceding equation can be squared to get x + 2 = x 2. Take x and 2 and subtract them from both sides of x + 2 = x^2. produces x^2 - x - 2 = 0. This equation's left side can be factored to get (x − 2)(x + 1) = 0. The answers to (x − 2)(x + 1) = 0 are x − 2 = 0, or x = 2, and x + 1 = 0, or x = −1, according to the zero product property.

The given equation is false when x = 2 is substituted, as per the definition of a main square root.

Therefore, x = 2 is not a solution. Entering x = -1 into the provided equation yields, which is accurate since −(−1) = 1. Therefore, the sole answer is x = −1.

Question 16

Option C is the right one. The cosine of the angle's complement equals the sine of the angle. This connection is exemplified by the Sin x° = cos (90° − x°) is the equation. Consequently, cos (90° − x°) must likewise equal an if sin x° = a.

Question 17

Option D is the right one. The point (x, y) at which y = 0 is the positive x-intercept of the graph of y = h(x). Since the height above is modeled by y = h(x), A y-value of 0 for the projectile's ground, measured in feet, must match the projectile's height when it is 0 feet above the ground, or when the projectile is on the ground. The positive x-intercept, (x, 0), indicates the moment the projectile strikes the ground since x reflects the amount of time after the bullet was launched.

Question 18

360 is the right response. A right rectangular prism's volume can be found by multiplying its length, width, and height. The volume is determined by multiplying the provided dimensions by $(4)(9)(10) = 360$ cubic centimeters.

Question 19

The right response is 2. The equation's left side, which can be expressed as $2(2x + 1)$, has a common factor of 2. dividing the two sides of this formula by two, resulting in $2x + 1 = 2$. Thus, $2x + 1$ has a value of 2. An alternative method is to subtract 2 from either side of the equation to get $4x = 2$. $x = 1 - 2$ is the result of dividing both sides of this equation by 4.

In the formula $2x + 1$, substituting $1 —2$ for x results in $2(1-2) + 1 = 2$.

Question 20

8 is the right response. The graph indicates that $f(x)$ has a maximum value of 2. Given that $g(x) = f(x) + 6$, the g-graph is just the f-graph pushed upward by half a unit. Consequently, $2 + 6 = 8$ is the greatest value of $g(x)$.

Question 21

4/3 is the right response. To solve for tanP, we need to understand the relationship between the sides of the triangle and the given trigonometric function sinR.

Given sinR=4/5 , we can interpret this as follows:

sinR=opposite/hypotenuse=4/5

This means that the side opposite angle R is 4 and the hypotenuse is 5.

In a right triangle, we can use the Pythagorean theorem to find the remaining side:

hypotenuse2=opposite2+adjacent2

5^2=4^2+adjacent25^2

25=16+adjacent^2

Adjacent^2=25–16=9

adjacent^2=√9=3

Now that we have all the sides of the triangle, we can find tanP:

tanP=opposite/adjacent=4/3

Question 22

The graph of the linear function f runs through the points (0, 3) and (1, 1), hence the solution is 2.5. The graph's inclination on the, function f is $\frac{1-3}{1-0} = -2$. It is assumed that the graphs of the linear functions g and f are perpendicular to one another. Thus, the negative reciprocal of −2 equals the slope of the function g's graph, which is $\frac{1}{-2} = \frac{1}{2}$ g(x) $= \frac{1}{2}$x + b, where b is a constant.

Math test – Module 2

Question 1
Option B is the right one. Taking three out of each side of the equation produces 3x = 24. x = 8 is obtained by dividing both sides of this equation by 3.

Question 2
The right answer is D. 140 cubits are equal to 140(7) palms, or 980 palms, since 1 cubit is equal to 7 palms.

Question 3
The proper choice is B. The answer to the following problem is 2n = 50 when both sides are multiplied by 5. When 50 is substituted for 2n in the formula 2n - 1, 50 - 1 = 49 is obtained.

Question 4
Option A is the right one. The primary, or non-negative, square root is represented by the square root symbol. Consequently, the equation Only when x is greater than or equal to 0 is the statement true. Therefore, the above equation cannot have −4 as a solution.

Question 5
The right answer is D. The graph's x-axis shows how long it took to remove the coffee from the heat source in minutes, and the temperature of the coffee is shown on the graph's y-axis in degrees Fahrenheit. When x = 0, the coffee was initially taken off of the heat source. The graph indicates that the y-value was just below 200°F when x = 0. 195 is the most accurate guess out of the provided answer selections.

Question 6
Option A is the right one. By dividing, one may determine the average rate of change in the coffee's temperature in degrees Fahrenheit per minute the number of minutes in the equivalent span of time that separates two recorded temperatures. Given that all of the time intervals are 10 minutes, the points with the biggest temperature differences have the largest average rate of change. The range of temperatures between 0 and 10 minutes has the biggest variation across the options.

Question 7
The correct choice is C. Since x = 100 is known, replacing x in triangle ABC with 100 yields two known angle measurements for this triangle. Any triangle has inner angles whose measures added together equal 180°. The third angle measure, 180° − 100° − 20° = 60°, is obtained by subtracting the two known angle measures of triangle ABC from 180°. This is the BCA angle's measurement. Angle DCE has a measure of 60° since vertical angles are

congruent. The third angle measure, 180° − 60° − 40° = 80°, is obtained by subtracting the two known angle values of triangle CDE from 180°. Consequently, y has a value of 80.

Question 8
Option A is the right one. The slope of the provided line represents the expense of every extra mile traveled. The line's slope can be computed by first locating two locations on the line, and then dividing the difference between the two spots' y-to-x changes. The slope equals to 2, using the coordinates (1, 5) and (2, 7). Consequently, the fare for every extra mile in the taxi is $2.00.

Question 9
Option D is the right one. There were 135 patrons at the gas station on Tuesday. The table displays the quantity of clients who did not buy fuel at the age of fifty. The likelihood that a client chosen at random that day did not purchase gasoline may be found by dividing the number of customers who did not purchase gasoline by the total number of customers. This figure is equal to $\frac{50}{135}$.

Question 10
The proper choice is B. It is known that 336 students participated in the survey. 1 of 336 found yields ((336) = 84, the quantity of identifying 1 of 336 yields = 112, which represents the number of sophomores, and freshmen. When these figures are deducted from the total number of chosen students, the number of juniors and seniors combined is 336 − 84 − 112 = 140.

Question 11
Option A is the right one. It is assumed that Plant C is 54 cm tall and that Plant A and Plant B have height ratios of 20 to 12. Let x represent Plant D's height. The value of x can be found via the percentage. When both sides of this equation are multiplied by x, the result is and when both sides are multiplied by 12, the result is 20x = 648. This equation's two sides can be divided by 20 to get x = 32.4 centimeters.

Question 12
Option D is the right one. It is assumed that one kilometer is roughly equal to 0.6214 miles. Let x be the corresponding number of kilometers up to 3.1 miles. The value of x can be found by using the proportion 1 kilometer. This problem can be solved by multiplying both sides by 3.1 to get x ≈ 4.99. This equates to about five kilometers.

Question 13
Option C is the right one. Let b be the number of shipments weighing 100 pounds, and let a be the number of packages weighing 120 pounds. Obviously, The packages' combined weight cannot exceed 1,100 pounds, as indicated by the inequality 120a + 100b ≤ 1,100. Additionally, it is assumed that the helicopter can carry a minimum of 10 parcels; this is represented by the inequality a + b ≥ 10. The number of 120-pound and 100-pound packages that the helicopter is permitted to transport is determined by the values of a and b that fulfill these two inequalities.

Reduce the quantity of 100-pound packages (b) in the helicopter in order to increase the quantity of 120-pound packages (a) in the aircraft.

Question 14
Option B is the right one. Subtracting $30,000 will reveal the difference between the machine's initial value and its value after ten years. 30,000 - $120,000 = 90,000 is the amount. It is assumed that during ten years, the machine's value will decrease by the same amount annually. The annual depreciation is $9,000, which can be calculated by dividing $90,000 by 10. Consequently, the machine loses value for a total of 9,000t dollars over a period of t years. The machine's value, denoted by v, is equal to its beginning value minus the amount of depreciation after t years, expressed in dollars (v = 120,000 − 9,000t).

Question 15
Option D is the right one. A linear equation has the slope-intercept form y = ax + b, where an is the equation's graph's slope and b is its value is the graph's y-coordinate for the y-intercept. The formula $a = \frac{y2-y1}{x2-x1}$ can be used to calculate the slope of the line for two ordered pairs, x1, y1) and x2, y2). When the two ordered pairs (2, 4) and (0, 1) are substituted into this formula, the result is $a = \frac{4-0}{2-0}$, which can be simplified to 3. When this number is substituted for an in the slope-intercept version of the equation, the result is y = 3/2 x + b. This equation generates 1 = 3/2 (0) + b when values from the ordered pair (0, 1) are substituted, indicating b.

Question 16
Option B is the right one. $4ax^2$ is the outcome of multiplying the binomials in the given expression. 4ax − 4x− 4 − x^2 + 4. Like terms added together result in 4ax^2 + 4ax − 4 −x^2. (4a − 1)x^2 + (4a − 4)x is the result of grouping by powers of x and factoring out their greatest common factors. Since this expression is known to be equal to bx, (4a − 1) x^2 + (4a − 4)x = bx. Given that there isn't an x^2 term on the right side of the equation, the coefficient of the x^2 term on the left side must be 0. Hence, 4a − 1 = 0 and 4a − 4 = b are obtained. 4a = 1 since 4a − 1 = 0. When 4a is substituted into the second equation, 1 − 4 = b is obtained, meaning that b = −3.

Question 17
Option C is the right one. 4w + 8t = 28 is the result of multiplying both sides of 2w + 4t = 14 by 2. subtracting 4w + 8t = 28 from the second provided equation gives either 3t = 3 or (28 − 25) from (4w − 4w) + (8t − 5t). t = 1 is obtained by dividing both sides of this equation by 3. In the equation 2w + 4t = 14, substituting 1 for t results in 2w + 4(1) = 14, or 2w + 4 = 14. This problem has two solutions: 2w = 10 when the number 4 is subtracted from both sides, and w = 5 when the two sides are divided by 2. In the expression 2w + 3t, substituting 1 for t and 5 for w results in 2(5) + 3(1) = 13.

Question 18
Option B is the right one. Considering that each serving of Crunchy Grain cereal supplies 5% of the daily potassium requirement for an adult, X servings equals X times the percentage. Five times the number of servings (x) is the percentage of potassium that an

adult should consume each day (p). Consequently, p = 5x can be used to describe the percentage of an adult's daily requirement of potassium.

Question 19

Option B is the right one. Option D is the right one. It is known that 240 calories are included in a cup of Crunchy Grain cereal. The entire caloric content of Jennifer's mixture is 270 calories per cup. Let ccc represent the quantity of Crunchy Grain cereal cups and sss the quantity of Super Grain cereal cups.

The formula 240c indicates how many calories there are in ccc cups of Crunchy Grain cereal, while 300s indicates how many calories there are in s cups of Super Grain cereal.

To solve this, we set up the equation for the total caloric content of the mixture:

240c+300s=270

Since the mixture is 1 cup, c+s=1. We can solve for ccc:

c=1−s

Substitute ccc in the caloric content equation:

240(1−s)+300s=270

Simplify:

240−240s+300s=270

Combine like terms:

240+60s=270

Solve for s:

60s=30

s=30

 s=12

So, Jennifer's mixture contains half a cup of Super Grain cereal.

Therefore, the correct answer is choice D, a half-cup.

Question 20

Option A is the right one. Crunchy Grains cereal has 0 calories per serving, hence the line has to start at (0, 0). Point (0, 0) is the source, denoted O. Furthermore, the calories increase by 250 with each serving. Consequently, the line needs to have a positive slope since the quantity of calories increases as the number of servings increases. Only option A displays a graph including a line that starts at the origin and slopes upward.

Question 21

Option D is the right one. The function h can be expressed as h(x) = abx since it is exponential, where b is the growth rate and an is the y-coordinate of the y-intercept. Given that the y-intercept's y-coordinate is d, the exponential function can be expressed as h(x) = dbx.

The only equation that satisfies these requirements is option D's.

Question 22

Option A is the right one. Finding the middle weight of the horses after sorting their weights from lightest to heaviest yields the median weight value derived from this weight list. Since it remains the lowest value, lowering the value for the horse with the lowest weight has no effect on the median.

PRACTICE TEST 2 ANSWERS

Reading and Writing test – Module 1

Question 1
Option C is the right one. The hatchlings' preference for the face-like pattern suggests that the attraction to such stimuli is likely an innate trait, rather than something learned through experience. Hence, "Thus, the attraction to face-like stimuli is likely innate rather than learned" is the correct choice.

Question 2
Option A is the right one. The presence of references to foreign customs and technologies in "The Chronicles of Kyoto" indicates that some entries were added after the initial compilation, reflecting later influences. Hence, "Thus, while its content largely predates modernization, 'The Chronicles of Kyoto' also contains later additions" is the correct choice.

Question 3
Option A is the right one. Since the study did not account for the physical difficulty of tasks, the results might mistakenly indicate differences in cognitive abilities that are actually due to task difficulty. Hence, "Thus, the results of the study could suggest differences in cognitive ability among the raccoons that may not actually exist" is the correct choice.

Question 4
Option D is the right one. The sentence should be: "To survive during periods of drought, the embryos of certain amphibians enter a state of suspended animation known as diapause." Hence, "Thus, enter" is the correct choice.

Question 5
Option C is the right one. The correct punctuation to separate two related ideas in this context is a comma: "The compound trimethylamine N-oxide (TMAO) helps proteins maintain their shape under such conditions and is found in high concentrations in the cells of deep-sea fish." Hence, "Thus, configurations, TMAO" is the correct choice.

Question 6
Option C is the right one. The sentence should be: "In 'Bitter in the Mouth,' the character of Linda experiences a form of synesthesia where words evoke tastes." Hence, "Thus, experiences" is the correct choice.

Question 7
Option C is the right one. The correct punctuation for possessive form is: "screw's threads." Hence, "Thus, screw's threads" is the correct choice.

Question 8
Option D is the right one. The correct punctuation to separate the clauses is a semicolon: "Researcher Dr. Lisa Kim of the University of Melbourne has suggested that the spider's distinctive coloration might actually attract prey; rather, it may be a strategy to lure in prey." Hence, "Thus, prey; rather," is the correct choice.

Question 9

Option C is the right one. The correct possessive form is: "playa's sediment mark the rocks'." Hence, "Thus, playa's sediment mark the rocks'" is the correct choice.

Question 10

Option B is the right one. The correct punctuation to separate the titles in a list is a comma: "Her novel 'Boy, Snow, Bird' is a retelling of Snow White, while her novel 'Gingerbread,' offers a twist on the tale of Hansel and Gretel." Hence, "Thus, Gingerbread," is the correct choice.

Question 11

Option C is the right one. The plot with unexpected twists that keep readers engaged is best described as "suspenseful." Hence, "Thus, the novel's plot is suspenseful, with unexpected twists that keep readers engaged until the very end" is the correct choice.

Question 12

Option B is the right one. The decision to "demolish" the old building would be met with praise and criticism from the community, indicating a significant change. Hence, "Thus, the committee's recommendation to demolish the old building was met with both praise and criticism from the community" is the correct choice.

Question 13

Option A is the right one. The importance of "clarity" in academic writing is emphasized, encouraging students to develop their own voice and style. Hence, "Thus, the teacher emphasized the importance of clarity in academic writing, encouraging students to develop their own voice and style" is the correct choice.

Question 14

Option B is the right choice. This option effectively highlights the significance of the mountains by mentioning their ranking as the highest and second-highest peaks in the world and their location in the Himalayan range. Hence, "The Himalayan range includes Mount Everest and K2, the highest and second-highest peaks in the world" is the most effective choice for emphasizing the importance of these mountains.

Question 15

Option C is the right one. The campaign resulting in a significant "increase" in sales indicates its effectiveness. Hence, "Thus, the marketing campaign was highly effective, resulting in a significant increase in sales" is the correct choice.

Question 16

Option B is the right one. The decision to "expand" the park would be met with widespread approval from residents. Hence, "Thus, the city council's decision to expand the park was met with widespread approval from residents" is the correct choice.

Question 17

Option A is the right one. A comprehensive overview of the topic makes the book an "invaluable" resource for students and professionals alike. Hence, "Thus, the book provides a comprehensive overview of the topic, making it an invaluable resource for students and professionals alike" is the correct choice.

Question 18

Option B is the right one. Jamie's primary concern in the scene is "getting to her meeting on time," as she is running late. Hence, "Thus, Jamie's primary concern is getting to her meeting on time" is the correct choice.

Question 19

Option B is the right one. The description of the quiet streets and distant sounds creates a "tranquil" atmosphere. Hence, "Thus, the atmosphere described in the scene is best characterized as tranquil" is the correct choice.

Question 20

Option B is the right one. The journal's entries are described as "colorful and imaginative," reflecting the detailed drawings and notes. Hence, "Thus, the journal's entries are primarily described as colorful and imaginative" is the correct choice.

Question 21

Option B is the right one. The primary focus of the scene is on Emma's "feeling of satisfaction" with the appearance of the bread. Hence, "Thus, the primary focus of the scene is on Emma's feeling of satisfaction" is the correct choice.

Question 22

Option B is the right one. The mood created by the vibrant carnival activities is best described as "festive," reflecting the excitement and enjoyment. Hence, "Thus, the mood of the fair is best described as festive" is the correct choice.

Question 23

Option C is the right one. Rachel's reaction to the letter, despite its heartfelt apologies, is one of "frustration," indicating she is not fully satisfied. Hence, "Thus, Rachel's reaction to the letter is one of frustration" is the correct choice.

Question 24

Option B is the right one. The description of the library's quiet reading room highlights its "calm and focused" setting, ideal for research. Hence, "Thus, the setting of the reading room is best described as calm and focused" is the correct choice.

Question 25

Option A is the right one. The description of the studio emphasizes the artist's "use of color" in the vibrant, abstract paintings. Hence, "Thus, the description of the studio emphasizes the artist's use of color" is the correct choice.

Question 26

Option B is the right one. The cozy atmosphere described by the crackling fire and rhythmic rain is best characterized as "warm and comforting." Hence, "Thus, the atmosphere inside Mark's house is best characterized as warm and comforting" is the correct choice.

Question 27

Option C is the right one. The purpose of the exhibition is to "educate the public about the town's history" through the display of historical artifacts. Hence, "Thus, the purpose of the exhibition is to educate the public about the town's history" is the correct choice.

Reading and Writing test – Module 2

Question 1

Option C is the right one. In 1995, the novel "Shadows in the Forest" was co-written by Maria Sanchez and David Lee, standing out as a prime example of cooperation in the literary world. Despite their successful collaboration, the experience strained their friendship, highlighting why many authors prefer to work solo. Hence, "In 1995, the novel 'Shadows in the Forest' was co-written by Maria Sanchez and David Lee, standing out as a prime example of cooperation in the literary world" is the correct choice.

Question 2

Option B is the right one. The current methods of mechanically recycling plastics are often deemed inadequate due to their environmental impact and the degradation of material quality that often ensues. However, chemist Sarah Taylor has pioneered a cleaner process of chemical recycling that transforms superabsorbent polymers from diapers into a valuable reusable adhesive. Hence, "The current methods of mechanically recycling plastics are often deemed inadequate due to their environmental impact and the degradation of material quality that often ensues" is the correct choice.

Question 3

Option D is the right one. Interruptions in the supply chain for semiconductors used in consumer electronics have challenged an analyst's prediction that sales of these devices will see significant growth in the near future. Although these delays are unlikely to negate her forecast entirely, they will almost certainly push back the timeline. Hence, "Although these delays are unlikely to negate her forecast entirely, they will almost certainly push back the timeline" is the correct choice.

Question 4

Option A is the right one. For her 2022 art installation, Harmony, artist Lisa Wu collaborated with musician and composer Jordan Rivers to create a piece that critics deemed truly captivating. They praised Wu for ingeniously converting a gallery space into a vibrant exhibit, projecting images of Rivers onto a large canvas and filling the room with the sound of his and other voices singing. Hence, "For her 2022 art installation, Harmony, artist Lisa Wu collaborated with musician and composer Jordan Rivers to create a piece that critics deemed truly captivating" is the correct choice.

Question 5

Option C is the right one. The organization's outreach program was designed to empower the community and provide essential services to those in need. Hence, "The organization's outreach program was designed to empower the community and provide essential services to those in need" is the correct choice.

Question 6

Option C is the right one. Despite facing numerous challenges, the team managed to complete the project ahead of schedule. Hence, "Despite facing numerous challenges, the team managed to complete the project ahead of schedule" is the correct choice.

Question 7

Option B is the right one. The new restaurant quickly gained popularity due to its diverse menu and excellent customer service. Hence, "The new restaurant quickly gained popularity due to its diverse menu and excellent customer service" is the correct choice.

Question 8

Option B is the right one. Text 1 presents an optimistic view of technological unemployment, arguing that while technology may eliminate some jobs, it creates new opportunities, leading to a net positive effect on employment. In contrast, Text 2 introduces studies suggesting that job displacement due to AI and automation may outpace job creation, potentially leading to widespread unemployment and inequality. This perspective directly challenges the optimistic view in Text 1 by presenting a more pessimistic outlook on the long-term effects of technological change on employment. Therefore, option B best describes how Text 2 relates to the argument in Text 1.

Question 9

Option C is the right one. The following text is adapted from Hannah Green's 1935 poem "Urban Nights in Spring." Night wears a garment All velvet soft, all violet blue... And over her face she draws a veil As shimmering fine as floating dew... And here and there In the black of her hair The subtle hands of Night Move slowly with their gem-starred light. Hence, "It uses an extended metaphor comparing night to a person" is the correct choice.

Question 10

Option D is the right one. According to historian Laura Martinez, Latina women played pivotal roles in the labor movement during the 1940s. During this time, manufacturing companies signed contracts to supply the United States military with essential goods. The increased production demands gave workers, many of whom were Latina women, greater bargaining power: they demanded better benefits, and employers, eager to meet contract deadlines, complied. Thus, labor activism became a platform for Latina women to assert their influence. Hence, "It offers more information about the workers discussed previously" is the correct choice.

Question 11

Option A is the right one. The following text is adapted from the short story "The Journey Home" by Sarah Williams, published in 1925. Ten-year-old Emma lived in a small village surrounded by dense woods. Her vivid imagination and love for daydreaming puzzled the village folk. A small river flowed just beyond her backyard, its banks lined with willows, oaks, and birches. The water was dotted with colorful lily pads. Emma loved to wander to the water's edge, toss in small twigs, and watch them drift downstream, dreaming of the distant lands they might reach and wishing she could follow them. Hence, "It elaborates on the scenery of a place Emma enjoys visiting" is the correct choice.

Question 12

Option B is the right one. The following text is adapted from Oscar Wilde's 1891 novel "The Picture of Dorian Gray." Dorian Gray is taking his first look at a portrait that Hallward has painted of him. Dorian passed listlessly in front of his picture and turned towards it. When he saw it he drew back, and his cheeks flushed for a moment with pleasure. A look of joy came into his eyes, as if he had recognized himself for the first time. He stood there motionless and in wonder, dimly conscious that Hallward was speaking to him, but not catching the meaning of his words. The sense of his own beauty came on him like a revelation. He had never felt it before. Hence, "He is captivated by his own likeness in the painting" is the correct choice.

Question 13

Option B is the right one. The novel "Whispering Pines" by Emma Roberts, published in 2005, is a rare example of partnership in contemporary literature. Roberts co-authored the book with her longtime friend, yet the process strained their relationship, underscoring why many authors prefer to write solo. Hence, "The novel 'Whispering Pines' by Emma Roberts, published in 2005, is a rare example of partnership in contemporary literature" is the correct choice.

Question 14

Option B is the right one. The traditional method of recycling aluminum cans is often seen as outdated due to the energy-intensive processes and environmental impact involved. However, engineer Paul Stevens has developed a new approach that significantly reduces energy consumption and improves efficiency. Hence, "The traditional method of recycling aluminum cans is often seen as outdated due to the energy-intensive processes and environmental impact involved" is the correct choice.

Question 15

Option C is the right one. Supply chain disruptions for raw materials in the automotive industry have put into question the assertion that the sector will see substantial growth this year. These interruptions are unlikely to invalidate the forecast completely, but they will definitely prolong the expected recovery period. Hence, "These interruptions are unlikely to invalidate the forecast completely, but they will definitely prolong the expected recovery period" is the correct choice.

Question 16

Option C is the right one. For her 2023 sculpture series Reflections, artist Maya Johnson collaborated with architect Daniel Park to create works that critics found truly innovative. They commended Johnson for transforming public spaces with interactive installations that engaged viewers on multiple levels. Hence, "For her 2023 sculpture series Reflections, artist Maya Johnson collaborated with architect Daniel Park to create works that critics found truly innovative" is the correct choice.

Question 17

Option A is the right one. Some biologists have argued that reptiles in the Triassic period were not a particularly diverse group. However, Dr. Elena Ramirez's research suggests that these ancient reptiles displayed a remarkable variety of forms and behaviors. Fossils found in Argentina reveal species with unique adaptations, such as Gliding Lizardus, which Dr.

Ramirez believes could glide between trees. Hence, "Some biologists have argued that reptiles in the Triassic period were not a particularly diverse group" is the correct choice.

Question 18
Option B is the right one. The novel "Silent Echoes," published in 2010 by Lisa Carter, is celebrated for its vivid use of language, which draws readers into the story's rich and atmospheric setting. Hence, "The novel 'Silent Echoes,' published in 2010 by Lisa Carter, is celebrated for its vivid use of language, which draws readers into the story's rich and atmospheric setting" is the correct choice.

Question 19
Option B is the right one. The entrepreneur's innovative approach to business has not only increased profits but also improved community relations. Hence, "The entrepreneur's innovative approach to business has not only increased profits but also improved community relations" is the correct choice.

Question 20
Option A is the correct choice because it demonstrates proper pronoun-antecedent agreement. The plural pronoun "them" matches the plural antecedent "utensils."
Option B is incorrect as the singular pronoun "this" does not align in number with the plural antecedent "utensils." Option C is also incorrect because the singular pronoun "that" fails to match the plural antecedent "utensils." Lastly, Option D is incorrect because the singular pronoun "it" does not agree in number with the plural antecedent "utensils."

Question 21
Option D is the right one. The council voted to implement the new policy immediately, despite concerns from some members about its potential drawbacks. Hence, "The council voted to implement the new policy immediately, despite concerns from some members about its potential drawbacks" is the correct choice.

Question 22
Option A is the right one. The artist's latest exhibition, which features a series of sculptures made from recycled materials, illustrates the importance of sustainability in modern art. Hence, "The artist's latest exhibition, which features a series of sculptures made from recycled materials, illustrates the importance of sustainability in modern art" is the correct choice.

Question 23
Option A is the right one. The company's decision to expand internationally was driven by a desire to increase market share. Hence, "The company's decision to expand internationally was driven by a desire to increase market share" is the correct choice.

Question 24
Option C is the right one. The politician's speech was characterized by emphatic statements and emotional appeals, aiming to rally support from the public. Hence, "The politician's speech was characterized by emphatic statements and emotional appeals" is the correct choice.

Question 25

Option A is the right one. The main advantage of the new software is its ability to increase productivity. Hence, "The main advantage of the new software is its ability to increase productivity" is the correct choice.

Question 26

Option C is the right one. Despite initial skepticism, the scientist's findings were eventually embraced by the broader scientific community. Hence, "Despite initial skepticism, the scientist's findings were eventually embraced by the broader scientific community" is the correct choice.

Question 27

Option A is the right one. The researcher's innovative method has the potential to revolutionize the field of biotechnology. Hence, "The researcher's innovative method has the potential to revolutionize the field of biotechnology" is the correct choice.

Math test- Module 1

Question 1

Option B is the right one. T = 15n + 12 gives the total T, in dollars, that Salim will pay for n tickets. This includes a one-time service fee as well as a per-ticket cost. Given the quantity of tickets Salim buys, 15n must equal the cost of n tickets in US dollars. Thus, the price per ticket must equal 15. At the same time, Salim will only be assessed the $12 fee once, regardless of the quantity of tickets he purchases. As a result, 12 must be the service charge's monetary amount.

Question 2

Option B is the right one. x pounds of Fertilizer A equals 0.6x pounds of filler materials since Fertilizer A comprises 60% filler materials by weight. In the same way, x pounds of fertilizer B has 0.4 y pounds of filler material in it. 240 pounds of filler materials are produced by combining x pounds of Fertilizer A and y pounds of Fertilizer B. Hence, 0.6x + 0.4y = 240 represents the total amount of filler materials, in pounds, in a mixture of x pounds of Fertilizer A and y pounds of Fertilizer B.

Question 3

Option C is the right one. When a complex number is expressed in the form a + bi, the real component of the number is denoted by a, and the imaginary part by b. Two complex numbers added together, Real and imaginary portions are added to find bi and c + di, respectively; that is, (a + bi) + (c + di) = (a + c) + (b + d)i. Consequently, 2 + 4) + (3 + 8)i = 6 + 11i is the total of 2 + 3i and 4 + 8i.

Question 4

Option A is the right one. The distributive property can be used to multiply the right side of the equation: P = (px + t)(px − t) Two by two − ptx + ptx − t^2. When similar terms are combined, p 2 x 2 − t 2 is obtained. When the right side of the equation is substituted with this expression, $4x^2 − 9 = p^2 x^2 − t^2$ is obtained, where p and t are constants. Only when 4 = p^2 and 9 = t^2 are true for all values of x does this equation hold true. 4 = p^2, so that either p = 2 or p = −2. As a result, only two of the possible answers for p could be the value provided.

Question 5

Option D is the right one. A line with slope m and y-intercept (0, b) represents the graph of the equation y = mx + b in the xy-plane, where m and b are constants. Consequently, the y = 2x - 5 graph in The xy-plane is a line with a y-intercept of (0, −5) and a slope of 2. A slope of two indicates that the value of y increases by two for every one increase in x. The only graph with a slope of two that crosses the y-axis at (0, −5) is the one in option D. Consequently, option D's graph has to be the right response.

Question 6

The answer is option A. Entering y = 18 as a given value into equation x=2/3 y provides x = (2/3) (18), which means x = 12. When x = 12, the value of the formula 2x − 3 is 2(12) − 3 = 21.

Option B is not correct. If 2x − 3 = 15, then x = 9 is obtained by adding 3 to both sides of the equation and dividing both sides by 2. It is incorrect to get the equation 2/3x by substituting 9 for x and 18 for y. Consequently, 2x − 3 cannot have a value of 15. Additionally, choices C and D are wrong. Like option B, let's say that 2x − 3 equals 12 or

Question 7

The correct choice is C. Based on multiplication properties, the formula n=(7h) l can be expressed as n= 7lh. Divide both sides of the equation by factor 7h to find the solution in terms of n and h. The result of solving this equation is n/7h.

Question 8

Option B is the right one. By drawing a link between the algebraic equation and the table, this question can be solved. The values of x and their related values are shown in each row of the table in t(x) as well as w(x). For example, x = 1 and the related numbers w(1) = −1 and t(1) = −3 are shown in the first row. The only row in the table with the attribute x = w(x) + t(x): 2 = 3 + (−1) is the row with x = 2. As a result, option B is the right response.

Question 9

Option C is the right one. The given equation's two numerical expressions can be reduced to $\sqrt{9}=3$ and $\sqrt{64} =8$, therefore alternative versions of the equation are $\sqrt{x} + 3 = 8$ or $\sqrt{x} = 5$. By squaring both sides of the equation x = 25.

Question 10

Option D is the right one. For four weeks, Jaime wants to log at least 280 miles per week on average. Jamie's objective can be represented if T is the total mileage he plans to ride his bicycle over the next four weeks. By means of the inequality symbolically: T ≥ 4(280) or 280 4 T ≜. Jamie will ride his bicycle for a total of miles during this time, which is the total of the distances he has already covered and has yet to cover. T thus equals 240 + 310 + 320 + x. This expression becomes 240 + 310 + 320 + x ≥ 4(280) when it is substituted into the inequality T ≥ 4(280). As a result, option D is the right response

Question 11

Option B is the right one. The parabola in the illustration opens upward, therefore the coefficient of x^2 in the formula y = ax^2 + c needs to be positive. Since a is positive and −a is negative, the graph of the equation y = −a(x − b)^2 + c will open downward as a parabola. Since x = b is the point at which y, c reaches its highest value, the vertex of this parabola is (b, c). Consequently, option B must be the response.

Question 12

The right answer is choice D. To simplify the expression

$(4x^2+6x)/(4x+2)$

First, factor out the greatest common factor in the numerator:

$4x^2+6x=2x(2x+3)$

So the expression becomes:

$(2x(2x + 3))/(4x + 2)$

Next, factor out the greatest common factor in the denominator:

$4x+2=2(2x+1)$

Now the expression is:

$(2x(2x+3))/(2(2x+1))$

We can cancel out the common factor of 2 from the numerator and the denominator:

$(x(2x+3))/(2x+1)$

Now, rewrite the expression:

$x+3x/2x+1$

Since none of the provided choices directly match this form, let's verify:

$x+1−2/(4x+2)$

To check if choice D is correct:

$x+1−2/(4x+2) =x+1−2/(2(2x+1))=x+1−1/(2x+1)$

After comparing the simplified forms, choice D simplifies correctly:

$x+1−2/(4x+2)$

Therefore, the correct answer is choice D.

Question 13

The right answer is choice A. To determine the value of t that would result in no true solutions, we need to analyze the quadratic equation:

2x^2 - 4x - t = 0

For a quadratic equation

ax^2 + bx + c = 0

to have no real solutions, the discriminant must be less than zero. The discriminant is given by b^2 - 4ac.

Here, a is 2, b is negative 4, and ccc is negative t.

Calculate the discriminant:

(−4)^2−4×2×(−t)=16+8t

For there to be no real solutions, the discriminant must be less than zero: 16+8t<0

Solve for t: 8t<−16

t<−2.

The only choice where t is less than negative 2 is: A) -3.

So, the correct answer is: A) -3.

Question 14

Option A is right. A shipment's number of containers shall weigh no more than 300 pounds. The total weight of fabric softener and detergent that the supplier supplies, expressed in pounds

can be calculated as follows: 7.35d for detergent and 6.2s for fabric softener; this is the weight of each container multiplied by the quantity of each type of container. Since 300 pounds is the maximum that this total can have, 7.35d + 6.2s <= 300. Additionally, the quantity of detergent containers should be greater than or equal to twice the quantity of fabric softener containers because the laundry service needs to purchase at least twice as many detergent containers as fabric softener containers. This is conveyed by inequality.

Question 15

Choice D is correct. The expression can be rewritten as $a^2 + ab + \frac{b^2}{4}$

Question 16

The right answer is choice B. To determine how many times the ball reached at least two feet in height, observe the graph and count the peaks that reach or exceed the two-foot mark.

From the graph:

1. The first peak reaches slightly above three feet.
2. The second peak reaches slightly above two feet.

There are two distinct peaks where the height of the ball is at least two feet. Therefore, the ball was at least two feet high after it was dropped:

Question 17

Option D is the right one. The right answer is choice D: 5.4%. To calculate the percentage increase:

1. Calculate the difference: $79.86 - $75.74 = $4.12
2. Divide the increase by the original amount: $4.12 / $75.74 = 0.05439 or 5.439%
3. Rounding to the nearest tenth of a percent gives 5.4% This matches option D.

Question 18

The right answer is 4. Let's approach this step-by-step:

1. We're given that a^b = 16
2. 16 can be expressed as 2^4
3. Therefore, a^b = 2^4
4. The largest possible value for b would be when a is at its smallest possible value, which is 2
5. So, 2^b = 2^4
6. This means b = 4 Therefore, the maximum value that b can have is 4.

Question 19

The right answer is 15/4 or 3.75. Let's solve the equation:

1. 2/3 t = 5/2
2. Multiply both sides by 3/2 to isolate t: t = (5/2) * (3/2)
3. Simplify: t = 15/4 = 3.75 Therefore, the value of t is 15/4 or 3.75.

Question 20

30 is the right response. Given that $B\overline{\overline{D}}$ is parallel to $\overline{A\overline{\overline{E}}}$ and that $C\overline{\overline{E}}$ intersects both segments in the given figure, angles BDC and AEC are corresponding angles and, as a result compatible. Since angle ACE and angle BCD are the same, they are also congruent. Triangle BCD and triangle ACE are comparable to each other if two of their angles are congruent to two of the other triangle's angles. Triangle ACE and triangle BCD have similar sides, hence their corresponding sizes are equal. Thus, $B\overline{\overline{D}}$ corresponds to $\overline{A\overline{\overline{E}}}$ and $C\overline{\overline{D}}$ correlates to $C\overline{\overline{E}}$ in triangles BCD and ACE.

Question 21

3 or 2 is the right response. The liters of each type of saline solution multiplied by the saline solution's percentage can be used to get the overall amount of saline solution, expressed in liters. 3(0.10), x(0.25), and (x + 3)(0.15) are obtained as a result, where x is the volume of a 25% saline solution in liters and 10%, 15%, and 25% are denoted by the numbers 0.10, 0.15, and 0.25, respectively. It follows that 3(0.10) + 0.25x = 0.15(x + 3) must be accurate. After dividing 0.15 by (x + 3) and multiplying 3 by 0.10, we get 0.30 + 0.25x = 0.15x + 0.45.

Question 22

The right response is 1/6 .166,.167, etc. A circle's circumference, C, is equal to 2πr, where r is the circle's radius. The circumference of the circle with radius 1 is C = 2(π)(1), or C = 2π. Divide the arc's length by the circumference to get $\pi 3 \div 2\pi$, which is the length of arc AB as a fraction of the circumference. The division can be expressed as follows: $\pi 3 \cdot 1\ 2\ \pi = 16$.

One alternative way to rewrite the fraction 1/6 is as.166 or.167.

Math test - Module 2

Question 1

The answer is option A. The stated formula $(2x^2)$ It is possible to rewrite $- 4) - (-3x^2 + 2x - 7)$ as $2x^2 - 4 + 3x^2 - 2x + 7$. When similar phrases are combined, $5x^2 - 2x + 3$.

Question 2

Option C is the right one. The locations of Paul and Mark throughout the race are indicated by the lines on the graph. Since there are 0 seconds remaining in the race when it begins, the y-intercept of the line showing Mark's location indicates how many yards Mark was away from Paul's starting position of 0 yards. Mark had a head since the line that depicts his position's y-intercept is at the grid line that lies halfway between 12 and 24.

Question 3

Option A is the right one. The first time period is represented by the leftmost segment in choice A, which depicts the snow accumulating at a specific rate; the second time period is represented by the middle segment, which is horizontal and indicates that the snow stopped accumulating; and the third time period is represented by the rightmost segment, which is steeper than the first segment and indicates that the snow accumulated at a faster rate than it did initially.

Question 4

Option D is the right one. The monthly charge, denoted by d, can be found using the equation 12d + 350 = 1,010. This equation has two sides, 350 from which we subtract to get 12d = 660, and when we divide both sides by 12, we get d = 55.

Question 5

The proper choice is B. The inequality can be split by 3 on both sides to get 2x − 3y > 4.

Question 6

The proper choice is C. The figure shows that 63% of survey participants acquire the majority of their medical information from a doctor, whereas 13% get it mostly online.

As a result, 912 out of the 1,200 study participants, or 76% of them, acquire their knowledge from the Internet or from doctors.

Question 7

Option D is the right one. The city council members desired to evaluate the views of every city inhabitant. The council ought to have employed a random selection procedure to get an impartial sample. plan to choose topics from among all city dwellers. A sampling bias was added into the study because all 500 city residents who participated had dogs. Not all city dwellers are represented in this sample.

Question 8

The proper choice is D. Thirteen individuals selected vanilla ice cream, based on the table. Eight of those individuals choose hot fudge as the topping. Consequently, 8 13 persons selected hot fudge as a topping out of those who selected vanilla ice cream.

Question 9

Option B is the right one. To determine the population density, we first need to calculate the land area by subtracting the water area from the total area: 92.1 square miles (total area) - 11.3 square miles (water area) = 80.8 square miles (land area).

Next, we divide the population by the land area to find the population density: 621,000 people / 80.8 square miles ≈ 7,690 people per square mile.

Therefore, the correct answer is B) 7,690.

Question 10

Option B is the right one. Let x be the total number of days on the second journey. Then, x + 43 is the total number of days that the initial voyage lasted. Given that the two journeys lasted 1,003 days in total, the equation x + (x + 43) = 1,003 had to hold. When like terms are combined, 2x + 43 = 1,003 is produced; x = 480 is obtained by solving for x.

Question 11

Option B is the right one. As may be seen below, adding the formulas side by side eliminates y.

$$7x + 3y = 8$$
$$6x - 3y = 5$$
$$\overline{13x + 0 = 13}$$

Question 12

Option D is the right one. The height rise of the sunflower over the period divided by the time is the average growth rate of the sunflower over that time. It can be said that this rate is where a and b stand for the first and last day of the time period, respectively. h (b) h (a) / ba. Given that the duration of each option is the same—21 days—it is possible to determine which time period the sunflower grew the least by looking at the overall growth throughout that duration. The sunflower had the least growth between days 63 and 84, based on the graph. Consequently, from day 63 to day 84, the sunflower's average growth rate was the lowest.

Question 13

Option B is the right one. As per the table, the sunflower's height measures 36.36 cm on day 14 and 131.00 cm on day 35. From day 14 until day 35, when the sunflower reached its peak changes at a rate that is almost consistent; the sunflower's height rises by about $\frac{131.00-36.36}{35-15}$ =4.5 cm each day.

Question 14

The right answer is choice B. The sunflower's growth rate is steady from day 14 to day 35, so we need a linear equation. We can calculate the rate of growth: On day 14: h = 4.5(14) - 27 = 36 cm On day 35: h = 4.5(35) - 27 = 130.5 cm This matches a steady growth rate of about 4.5 cm per day, which is represented by the equation h = 4.5t - 27.

Question 15

The right answer is choice D. We can verify this by checking the equation for each pair of x and y values: For x = 1: y = 7/2(1) - 3/4 = 11/4 For x = 2: y = 7/2(2) - 3/4 = 25/4 For x = 3: y = 7/2(3) - 3/4 = 39/4 And so on. The equation y = 7/2x - 3/4 correctly relates y to x for all given values.

Question 16

The right answer is choice B. In similar triangles, the ratios of corresponding sides are equal. BC/AB in triangle ABC corresponds to DF/DE in triangle DEF. Therefore, BC/AB = DF/DE, which can be rearranged to BC/AB = DF/EF.

Question 17

The right answer is choice B. Starting with the riser-tread formula 2h + d = 25, we can solve for h: 2h = 25 - d h = (25 - d) / 2 h = 1/2(25 - d) This matches option B.

Question 18

The right answer is choice C. Given the constraints: d ≥ 9 (tread depth at least 9 inches) h ≥ 5 (riser height at least 5 inches) Using the formula 2h + d = 25, we can substitute d ≥ 9: 2h + 9 ≤ 25 2h ≤ 16 h ≤ 8 Combining this with h ≥ 5, we get: 5 ≤ h ≤ 8 This matches option C.

Question 19

The right answer is choice C. Let's approach this step-by-step:

1. The total climb is 9 feet = 108 inches

2. For an odd number of steps, let's say there are 2n+1 steps, where n is an integer
3. Given the riser height h is between 7 and 8 inches: 7 < h < 8
4. Total climb = number of steps × riser height: 108 = (2n+1)h
5. Solving for n: n = (108/h - 1)/2
6. For n to be an integer, 108/h must be odd
7. The only value of h between 7 and 8 that makes 108/h odd is 7.2 (108/7.2 = 15)
8. With h = 7.2, we can use the riser-tread formula to find d: 2(7.2) + d = 25 d = 25 - 14.4 = 10.6 Therefore, the tread depth must be 10.6 inches, which matches option C.

Question 20

The right answer is option C. To solve (x-6)(x+0.7)=0, either x-6=0 or x+0.7=0. From x-6=0, we get x=6. From x+0.7=0, we get x=-0.7. The question asks for the total of these solutions: 6 + (-0.7) = 5.3 This matches option C: 5.3.

Question 21

The right answer is choice D. The sample data only provides information about largemouth bass, not about all fish in the pond. The sample shows that 30% of the largemouth bass weighed more than two pounds. We can reasonably extrapolate this to the population of largemouth bass in the pond, but not to all fish species. Therefore, the best supported conclusion is that about 30% of all largemouth bass in the pond weigh more than two pounds.

Question 22

The right answer is choice B. To find the median, we need to arrange the electoral votes in order and find the middle value. There are 21 states, so the median will be the 11th state when ordered. Ordering the states by electoral votes: 10,10,10,10,11,11,11,11,12,13,15,15,15,17,20,21,21,27,31,34,55 The 11th state (the median) has 15 electoral votes. This matches option B.

☆ ☆ ☆ ☆ ☆

SUBMIT A REVIEW

Did these pages help, inspire, or bring you value in any way? If so, we'd love to hear your thoughts through an honest review on Amazon. Your feedback is incredibly valuable to us!

It's very simple and only takes a few minutes:

1. Go to the "My Orders" page on Amazon and search the book.
2. Select "Write a product review".
3. Select a Star Rating.
4. Optionally, add text, photos, or videos and select Submit.

CONCLUSION

As you reach the end of this guide, take a moment to think back on your journey in the past few months while preparing strategically with the Digital SAT® Study Guide. When you first began your preparation, the new exam format and abundance of resources may have seemed overwhelming. However, by following the step-by-step approach outlined here. From creating a schedule and setting goals on the Dashboard to immersing yourself in each Lesson sequentially practicing rigorously under different conditions and focusing on improving weaker areas. You've armed yourself with effective learning and test-taking strategies. You've gained experience by applying these methods through practice questions, adjusting your strategies based on detailed feedback to address any weaknesses continuously. With each practice session, your speed, endurance, and ability to tackle problems improved noticeably.

Over time, concepts shifted from being unfamiliar to becoming nature as you revisited them in portions designed for better retention and recall under pressure. Your capability to methodically work through exams within time limits while minimizing mistakes now reflects a grasp of fundamental principles.

Above all, by reflecting on your progress guided by score analyses, you've cultivated a growth mindset crucial for success not just on the SAT® but also, in future endeavors. Evaluating strengths and areas needing improvement objectively helped you focus your study time where it mattered most. Staying positive despite setbacks kept you motivated to keep refining your skills. This perseverance is crucial, for navigating challenges in education and career paths. You feel confident that your hard work has prepared you well for whatever comes not for a single test.

As you enter the weeks of preparation, reflect on how you've come since the beginning but strive to avoid becoming complacent by sticking to your proven study routines. Reviewing explanations from practice tests diligently is key to maintaining focus. During breaks, it's important to relax without dwelling on mistakes. Taking time off on weekends is essential for performing at your best when it counts. While waiting for results, visualizing success helps you stay calm and collected during the exam. After submitting your work, take time to reflect on the process with a mindset. Analyzing your scores objectively helps you identify areas where you can improve without being too hard on yourself comparing them to performances.

Regardless of the outcome, acknowledge that there's always room for growth and improvement if you aim for scores or further education opportunities in the future. Celebrating your dedication and resilience in facing challenges is important. They have only made you stronger. Always stay in a learning mindset to drive yourself towards accomplishments using data to guide your progress in endeavors. Don't forget to give feedback to help improve resources for the benefit of those who will take tests after you. Show appreciation to everyone who has supported you by sharing study materials or words of encouragement. Share proven strategies to empower others with the confidence that you have gained by utilizing tools. Your continuous contributions help create a cycle of growth and improvement.

When faced with challenges, remember the resilience you have developed and have faith in your potential through a commitment to learning and serving others. Exciting opportunities lie ahead when you apply the strengths you have acquired.

Made in the USA
Las Vegas, NV
06 February 2025

17621311R00116